PANIC, PASSION AND POWER

Lessons from a Management Journey

Paul Dyer and Brian Thomas

Published by Stream Limited

Paul Dyer & Brian Thomas have asserted their rights under the Copyright, Designs and Patents Act, 1988 to be identified as the authors of this work.

Stream Limited
Churchill House, 27 Little Marlow Road
Marlow, Bucks SL7 1HA

A CIP catalogue record for this book is available from the British Library

Typeset by Stream Limited, Marlow, Bucks
Printed and bound by Anthony Rowe Limited, Chippenham, Wiltshire.

ISBN 978-0-9556594-0-9

*Dedicated to the people who have built
Towergate into the company
it is today and to those who will take it
forward into tomorrow.*

Contents

Introduction

What does it take to be an effective manager and run a successful business?

These questions have occupied the minds of large numbers of people for long periods of time. In the past twenty years alone there has been a glut of business and management books published with the explicit claim to having found *the answers*. Such books are eagerly devoured by managers in all sectors. Public, Private, Charitable, Voluntary, Military, Health, Manufacturing, Services … the list is practically endless.

Essentially there are four genres of management book on offer:

First there's the *'Business Management is Very Very Complex'* variety which commonly recommend the application of fashionable or obscure scientific theories to business and management contexts. Typical titles include *'Quantum Organizations: A New Paradigm for Achieving Organizational Success and Personal Meaning'* and *'Leadership and the New Physics'* both of which apply Quantum Mechanics and Chaos Theory to business challenges (Chaos Theory and Quantum Mechanics are big in this genre).

In stark contrast to the first type is the *'Business Management is Very Very Simple'* genre whose authors usually imply that management and business success comes from understanding certain 'secrets' (secrets that, naturally, their books will reveal!) Secrets are big in management writing too - typing the word 'secrets' into the search engine of Amazon's Business and Finance book section delivered

(January 2007) 1,526 titles on offer, including:

'*29 Leadership Secrets from Jack Welch*', '*Secrets of the Millionaire Mind*' and (a particular favourite of ours) '*I've Seen a Lot of Famous People Naked, and They've Got Nothing on You: Business Secrets from the Ultimate Street-smart Entrepreneur*'.

'Secrets' of business success clearly sell (particularly when the author suggests there is a finite number of them) e.g. '*The Twelve Secrets of Phenomenal Leadership*' or '*The Twenty-one Secrets of Successful Face-to-Face Negotiating*'.

The third type of business book is based on the life and experiences of successful managers and entrepreneurs, the '*How I Did it*' genre, which include titles such as '*Jack: Straight from the Gut*': Jack Welch (again) '*How to Get Rich*': Donald Trump, and '*Business the Richard Branson Way*'.

Lastly there's the mind-numbingly-simplistic-to-utterly-loopy variety that includes titles such as '*Feng Shui and Destiny for Managers*'; '*The Astrological Manager*' and '*Who Moved my Cheese?*'

To be fair, the thoughtful manager will probably benefit from reading careful selections from each of the four genres. And this fact neatly encapsulates the central problem. There is in reality no one-shot-sure-to-succeed pathway to management and business success. It isn't about applying Chaos Theory, knowing arcane secrets, emulating successful leaders or locating the cheddar. Rather there is a little of all involved. Plainly put, there is no *guaranteed* formula for achieving managerial or business success. What worked for Jack Welch and Richard Branson won't necessarily work for you because you're not Jack or Richard and you're not going to be working with the people and circumstances they worked with. But lessons can certainly be learned from the experiences and operating strategies of remarkably successful leaders and entrepreneurs.

Likewise we can usefully apply relevant scientific principles to business contexts and use practical psychological knowledge and appropriate metaphors to better understand the business and management challenges we face as fallible, normal, human beings.

This book will attempt to synthesise the more relevant aspects of all four approaches. In doing so we will analyse the core values, operating strategies and management principles underpinning the remarkable growth of a highly innovative UK financial services company: *The Towergate Partnership*.

In tandem with this biographical focus we will also include pertinent academic theories, highly practical 'coalface' business techniques and lastly some (hopefully) relevant operational metaphors.

The Towergate story from its creation in 1997

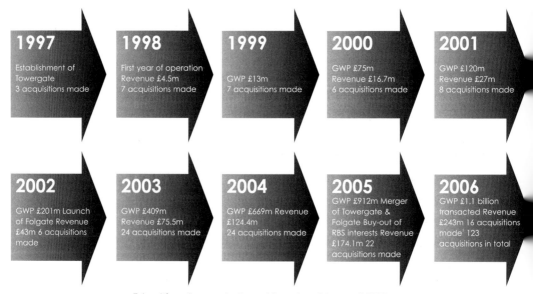

Extract from Towergate Annual Report and Account 2006

At Towergate we believe that insurance is very much a 'people business'. However, ultimately it is the numbers that show the strength of an organisation and give reassurance to shareholders, customers, intermediaries, insurers, employees and the great causes we support.

Here are some of our numbers:

No.1 we are Europe's largest independent insurance intermediary

£1.25billion gross written premium controlled[1]

£174million total 2005 income

40% growth in income 2005 v 2004

£61m 2005 pre-tax profit[2]

4000 agencies and outlets distributing our products

110 acquisitions successfully integrated

190 insurance products – the widest range in the market

100 offices across the UK[3]

3047 exceptional people making things happen[3]

£500,000 raised for Help the Hospices and other good causes

1 2005 on annualised basis
2 Earnings before interest, tax, depreciation, directors' bonuses and amortisation
3 As at 30th June 2006

Extract from Towergate Annual Report and Account 2006

In one respect therefore the bad news is that there is no guaranteed *formula* for managerial or business success. The good news however is that there certainly is a *recipe*. In this brief account we will describe what we believe to be the essential ingredients of that recipe, how best they should be combined however is the reader's prerogative entirely.

A Note on Content and Style

Writing an experience-based business book (even a relatively brief account such as this) is a tricky undertaking and we have approached the challenge with all due trepidation. The history of business publishing has repeatedly indicated that singling out particular companies or individuals as exemplars of good business or management practice can be very bad news indeed.

One of the most successful business books of all time: *In Search of Excellence: Lessons from America's Best-run Companies* (*Tom Peters and Robert H Waterman: 1982*) cited a number of then-prominent companies as 'having got the essentials for on-going success exactly right'. In fact many of those companies subsequently performed badly and in some cases disastrously. It was as if the citing process itself generated a business equivalent of the so-called 'curse of *Hello!*' magazine; the alarming tendency for 'golden couples' to hit serious difficulties within eighteen months or so of having their idyllic photographs appear within those hallowed pages!

Therefore tempting the fates and consequently shooting ourselves in the foot (or some place far worse) is definitely not our intention. Also, as the Roman philosopher and proto-business-guru Maximus Remunerus remarked many centuries ago, '*nobody likes a smart-arse*'. That astute observation has also remained firmly centre-stage throughout the process of putting this book together. Therefore we offer what follows very much in a spirit of exploration rather than exhortation.

This is definitely not a 'how to do it' manual written by 'experts' for the general edification of 'ordinary' folk. It is a brief account of a business journey; the trials and tribulations involved, the narrow squeaks and holes-in-one, the effects on key players, the lessons learned and general principles gleaned which are offered as hopefully being of interest and maybe of practical use to others who may venture on similar journeys.

We have three 'audiences' in mind. First, staff at all levels within Towergate who may be interested to know more on how the business actually got to where it is! Second, managers and aspiring managers who wish to better understand the 'cut and thrust' involved in growing and managing a fundamentally new business entity and thirdly those generally interested in business theories and management research.

We hope there will be something of interest for all. Our overriding aim however is to stimulate thought on the key challenges facing real managers and real leaders in a wide range of practical business contexts.

A Note on Writing Style:

The narrative of the book is mainly taken from Thomas's perspective. The observations, theories, lessons learned and ideas expressed however are a collective endeavour.

CHAPTER 1

Beginnings

I returned, and saw under the sun, that the race is not to the swift, nor the battle to the strong, neither yet bread to the wise, nor yet riches to men of understanding, nor yet favour to men of skill; but time and chance happeneth to them all.

Ecclesiastes 9:11

Time and Chance

The quotation above reminds us that success, be it in business or elsewhere, is not always the result of brilliant strategy, dazzling tactics, extensive knowledge or general all-encompassing 'intelligence' alone. Occasionally it may be, but most often it just isn't. On the other hand it is rare for an individual or business to succeed solely on the back of pure chance either.

There is an inevitable ability-chance balance involved in all ventures, successful or otherwise, and it is wise to recognise this. The balance may vary from situation to situation but it is a fact of life that good or poor fortune will play their part in the development of any undertaking. Despite this fact many management books appear to be seeking the 'golden rules' of organisational achievement, the blueprint for guaranteed business success. It is our belief that there are no such rules and no such blueprint. There are certainly lessons to be learned from successful and unsuccessful businesses and there are definitely management approaches we can utilise that will shorten the odds of us succeeding. But, as we shall see later, business is frequently a 'messy business' and the most logical plans and rigorous strategies can fall foul of the unexpected and the coincidental. As Britain's former prime minister Harold Macmillan once famously declared when asked to define what were the key factors influencing successful or unsuccessful political careers; 'events, dear boy, events.'

Time, chance and events have certainly influenced Towergate's establishment and subsequent growth as we will see, but first we would like to offer some practical examples that will hopefully flesh out the key points we wish to make about time and chance.

Imagine for a moment that you had set yourself up in

business as a mobile ice-cream vendor at the beginning of April 2005. If you had, you would have done so immediately prior to the hottest UK summer since records began in the late 1800's which was something of a surprise to the weather-wonks as 2005 was not an 'El Nino' year like 1998, the previous record-holder.

So, lucky old ice-cream-seller you!

Had you established your business exactly one year earlier however, in April 2004, you would then have been confronted with one of the wettest summers on record (again a rather unexpected event) with over a hundred severe weather warnings issued during the month of August alone – normally the peak of the ice-cream consumption season.

So a jobseeker's allowance would probably have constituted your entrepreneurial reward for that particular venture! Weather-dependent businesses are clearly tricky entities and their success or otherwise is heavily influenced by luck.

But what roles do intelligence and chance play in other business ventures?

Consider the following situation: imagine you are the CEO of a company that manufactures consumer electrical goods and you have personally sanctioned the (costly) development of a revolutionary new device. Your marketing department has investigated the potential uptake of the prototype (through focus groups, predictive random samplings etc) and the news is not good. Their considered opinion is that the device will not sell in sufficient numbers to justify its development and manufacturing costs, partly because it is too revolutionary for the current market and partly because you personally (in their view) have fixed the selling price way too low. Even the design team set up to develop the product is openly sceptical of its commercial possibilities. On top of all this your wife/husband/partner does not like the gadget one bit and, to add insult to injury, the marketers have sanctioned a name for it that is, in your considered opinion, truly awful (they did this while you were abroad on business and the cost of reversing their decision would now be prohibitive).

So, faced with the above situation, what would you do?

What the actual CEO did (and he faced the exact situation described) was to personally authorise a manufacturing run at considerable cost, stick with the relatively low selling price, stick with the name he hated because it was too costly to change it by then, and to go boldly forth! Why? Partly because he and a sixteen year-old relative of his loved the gadget to bits and they believed the sceptics had it wrong.

Who was the CEO?

Akio Morita of the Sony Corporation.

And the gadget?

The Sony Walkman (Morita detested the name 'Walkman' he wanted to call it the 'Walking Stereo' – so a bit of good fortune he was away then!)

As we now know, the Sony Walkman went on to become a truly global phenomenon that made the company hundreds of millions of dollars. The question worth reflecting upon of course is this – was Morita's decision to proceed (completely justified as it turned out) just a lucky throw, or did it have something to do with business intelligence?

We believe (in this particular instance at least) that it was primarily the latter. Sometimes the number-crunchers and research-nerds get it wrong and battle-hardened managers and quirky sixteen year-olds (who was the Walkman aimed at after all?) get it right.

The principal objection of the Walkman nay-sayers was that people would not be prepared to pay for a tape-player (this was pre-CD times remember) that did not also record music. But Morita believed that his target audience's desire to take their music with them wherever they went would outweigh this deficit. He was right. Sometimes people don't know what they want until they see it and feel it and use it, or see others using it. Morita had a gut feeling about the Walkman, a feeling predicated on years of experience in consumer electronics. His gut feeling told him it was the right time for the Walkman and he consequently took the chance. Time and chance.

Occasionally, just occasionally, the appropriate business approach can be 'Ready … Fire … Aim!' If you really have genuine business nous that is!

Time, chance and gut feelings have played their due part in the Towergate story too. In the early nineteen-nineties Peter Cullum and Paul Dyer were safely ensconced in the corporate citadels of ITT London and Edinburgh. ITT London & Edinburgh, in common with all ITT business units, had a strong discipline in strategic management. No decisions were taken without comprehensive business planning and close attention to the numbers – an environment in which Cullum naturally thrived. It has to be said that this was an unusual culture in the industry at that time.

Despite these internal strengths, Cullum, with his customary drive to push any business 'to do even better', was leading (or more accurately trying his best to lead) a company-wide revolution aimed at refocusing key business activities on external customers rather than internal processes (an internal focus was de-rigueur in the Insurance industry at that time and unfortunately remains far too common to this day). Dyer was actively assisting Cullum's drive for improved customer focus and also waging his own private war on the incomprehensibility of much Insurance documentation, a struggle that would ultimately lead to an award from the Plain English campaign, the first for Home Insurance given to an

Insurance company in the UK. Both men were pushing hard for change.

And then something pivotal happened.

Cullum describes the event as a turning point in the emotional relationship that existed between himself and the company he had committed his efforts to. It was nothing dramatic in terms of status, remuneration or position, rather it was a subtle shift in the unwritten rules, the 'psychological contract' if you like, that underpins all important human relationships.

Partly as a result of this perceived shift Cullum began to question what he really wanted to do with the rest of his working life. The insights he had gained through completing his MBA at Cass Business School (formerly City Business School, with its central focus on Risk Analysis) combined with the financial hammering that he (along with many others) had recently taken as a Lloyds 'name' put him in the frame of mind for serious change. What was becoming increasingly clear to Cullum was that a large proportion of his peers did not give much attention to the numbers. The losses at Lloyds were only a part of a decade of financial disasters that had seen the destruction of £23 billion in value (before investment income) from the UK insurance market.

That was the time … and then came the chance.

Economic Insurance, based in Sittingbourne, Kent, was a small UK insurer that had survived almost to the end of the twentieth century (even allowing for the fact that it had been involved in insuring such risks as part of the Titanic) but *almost* was the key word. In the early nineteen-nineties Economic was set firmly in the departure lounge of business life. Someone quite special would be required to lead it back to the check-in gates let alone the safety of the concourse. Enter Peter Cullum.

Cullum took a huge gamble in accepting the headhunters' requests to take on Economic. His position at ITT London and Edinburgh was solid, his reputation as an iconoclastic (some said 'bloody dangerous') but quite brilliant entrepreneurial maverick meant that his corporate star would inevitably rise. And Sittingbourne was certainly not the City of London! But for Cullum a contract was a contract, written on paper or agreed in principle. He also had a gut feeling that it was time for real change. So he upped sticks and took on Economic.

Economic Insurance

Economic's parent company, Danish Insurer Hafnia, gave Cullum fairly free rein to do what he thought necessary – within clear financial boundaries – to pull the company away from the precipice and manage it back to profitability (although he quickly spotted the presence of a head office 'spy' in the woodwork!)

Cullum hit the ground running.

First he needed to understand the fundamentals of the business. So, as ever, he looked hard at the numbers and he asked very difficult questions. An ability to grasp business numbers and challenge long-held assumptions have been enduring traits of the Cullum management 'method' over the years. In many ways he reminded Thomas of a past academic mentor who, when faced with any assertion that was not backed up with relevant numbers, would throw out the riposte;

'without data you're just somebody else with an opinion.'

Opinion is fine in many contexts, and in some situations opinion is practically all there is, but as far as gauging the health of a business is concerned, Cullum has always gone for the numbers. He has an eye for data interpretation and a talent for anomaly-spotting that sometimes borders on the uncanny. No-one takes half-baked or massaged business numbers to Peter Cullum and lives to tell the tale!

The numbers Cullum saw at Economic, and the answers he got to the hard questions he asked did not fill him with joy. Economic's management had products in markets totally dominated by the giant players in the UK and their lack of muscle mean that they were continually being hammered. It was a strategic mess.

Although the company had its normal share of able and less able staff, most were competent and committed. The central problem however was that too many were competent at the wrong things and committed to the wrong goals. There was a marked lack of clarity and focus to the business. Many people were working hard but going backwards. The ills of Economic arc, unfortunately, endemic to many businesses to this day.

Broadly speaking the major problems at Economic included:

• Erroneous assumptions concerning the most profitable lines of business to be in. At Economic the long-held assumption was that High Value commercial insurance was the most profitable track and Personal Lines insurance controlled by scheme brokers the least profitable. Cullum looked at the numbers and found this assumption to be one hundred and eighty degrees out of kilter.

• Individuals often assumed (erroneously) that they had a shared and agreed understanding of the technical terms used in the business. For example at Economic many line managers would conflate 'contribution' (which was essentially premium in) with 'profitability'. As a consequence they frequently did not allocate their operational expenses to their product lines but equated raw premium with company profit. This naturally led to very erroneous notions regarding the true state of the company's finances. Overall the financial focus was heavily top-line driven with little or no appreciation or interest in bottom-line impact.

- Economic was managed reactively rather than proactively and there was a marked tendency to 'count the paperclips' rather than address serious commercial challenges. There was no clear strategic direction, little if any focused marketing and an over-reliance on 'windfall' opportunities somehow coming along. By and large sales and marketing worked hard but their efforts were more akin to carpet bombing than laser-precision targeting, what Thomas describes as 'spray-and-pray marketing'. Sales volumes were often considered more important than actual quality of business won and sales was the dominant culture in the company.

- Economic was essentially a business comprised of 'silos', quasi-autonomous operating units (underwriting, claims, marketing, IT etc) that engaged in little if any productive cross-communication or proactive co-operation. In fact there was a palpable sense of hostility between many of the various 'camps' with each assuming the unofficial mantle of 'most effective department in the company.' This 'turfism' severely limited the company's ability to innovate and frequently resulted in missed business opportunities and unnecessary bottom-line costs. When Cullum became MD the Company had a £40 million premium income yet returned a £10 million loss! This was largely because management was caught out by the UK housing crash which slaughtered one of its key product lines – mortgage indemnity insurance.

- Something of an historic division existed between 'management' and 'staff' at Economic. Managerial staff had traditionally been seen as the 'brains' of the organization and non-managerial staff as its 'hands'. The unspoken rule being that managers 'thought' while staff 'did'.

Cullum immediately set about rectifying these ills and also set about persuading Dyer to leave L&E and join him in the venture. After a couple of gentle appeals, a few heavier onslaughts and then one of the 'brave-new-world-final-frontier' motivational spiels that Cullum is renowned for, Dyer succumbed.

Now they were both at Economic. The key organisational ills had been identified, the basic remedies (essentially the medicine Cullum had attempted to administer in his previous company) were known, the implementation plan was drawn up and the journey to profitability was about to commence in deadly earnest. Things were looking good. Then there was an event.

Hafnia went bust!

Economic's parent company succumbed to acquisition overload just ahead of a stock-market crash and earned itself the dubious accolade of becoming the largest financial collapse ever seen in Scandinavia.

Cullum and Dyer went through all seven stages of the catastrophe-reaction curve in pretty short order (there wasn't a great deal of time available for navel-gazing or self-pity, even allowing for the fact that Dyer had left a secure career only weeks before) then they started thinking about what, if anything, they could possibly do. If they did nothing Economic would almost inevitably fold and its business be absorbed by one or more of the giants. This, at first glance, seemed the most realistic outcome.

And then Cullum floated the idea of a management buyout.

Dyer, for one, was stunned. No-one in the Economic team, Cullum included, had any practical experience of raising venture capital of the stature required for a company MBO. Who would they go to? What business case would they present? What would Economic's existing distributors do? What about retaining key staff? How much personal risk would the team be required to take? No-one really knew what the answers to these questions would be (fortunately, in the case of the personal risks that would ultimately materialise, otherwise everyone with the exception of Cullum would have had serious reservations about going forward).

A key factor influencing the ultimate decision to go ahead with the MBO was the strong belief, based on Cullum's analysis of the core business challenges, that Economic could be turned around and brought back to profitability. But the most important factor, by a very wide margin indeed, was Cullum's commitment, drive and out-and-out leadership. Everyone involved in the MBO attested to the fact that they could not imagine anyone other than Peter Cullum having the presence or sheer confidence to convince them that buying Economic and turning it around was a viable and rational proposition. So, armed with the Economic team's agreement, Cullum set out to raise some serious money.

After a tremendous amount of hard work, numerous dead ends, having to bounce back from venture capital refusals (remember this was a company that had reported a £10 million loss the year Cullum took charge – although it was profitable two years later!) and an ability to keep going despite setbacks, Cullum's trajectory eventually intersected with that of Candover, a highly innovative venture capital company founded in 1980.

Candover's operating philosophy matched Cullum's personal profile exactly;

'At Candover we back people, not businesses. So we

choose to work with ambitious, entrepreneurial people whose vision matches our own.'

Source: www.candover.co.uk

While he was involved in the intense negotiations necessary to secure financial backing from Candover, Cullum also needed to keep Economic's key intermediaries and customers on board, if any of them abandoned ship the bid was doomed. This he did through sheer bloody-mindedness and a refusal to countenance anything other than success. Armed (as ever) with the business numbers and a clear recovery strategy, Cullum's ability to communicate his vision in such a way as to totally convince others of its veracity played a (probably the) vital role.

Economic's major distributors and customers gave Cullum a (time-limited) go-ahead to raise the necessary capital for the MBO – and then Candover came on board with the cash.

Sounds easy? It wasn't!

Everyone involved in the MBO worked literally day and night to make it happen. There were times when chance lobbed seemingly lethal bad-luck grenades into the bunker and all heads went down, Cullum's included. But people would bounce back, pick themselves up and find yet another escape route from yet another apparently impenetrable maze. The experience taught everyone involved the vital need for persistence in facilitating any sort of major success. And in this case the challenge was huge. Cullum had to solve the outstanding liabilities attaching to the Mortgage Indemnity book of business and he travelled all over the country negotiating with various leaders to agree terms to finalise the Company's exposure to continuing losses. Finality was key.

Cullum is never happier than when he is negotiating, whether from a position of strength or not! There were times when the brinkmanship he employed was breathtaking. Dyer watched in awe as Cullum often engaged in pure theatre to cajole, convince, pressurise and finally get a settlement that would confirm the liabilities Economic had to carry on into the MBO.

In December 1993 the necessary MBO funding was in place and Cullum and his small team were able to refocus their efforts on what was, even prior to the collapse of Hafnia, a pretty formidable challenge in its own right: turning Economic around. As Hafnia was under considerable duress and the sale of Economic (in their eyes at least) had become something of a sideshow. The result was that Cullum and his team managed (through some incredibly deft negotiations) to pay only £6.5 million for a Net Asset Value of £13 million.

A strong suit

Post Magazine 1994

"Poker players should steer clear of Peter Cullum, Economic's managing director. He has developed the perfect poker face after watching the masters of dead pan – the venture capitalists – at work, while the company went through a management buyout."

Through hard work, clear leadership, some pretty ruthless culling of staff at all levels (Cullum, like all successful business leaders, does not flinch from taking very hard decisions) and a total focus on the fundamental drivers of profitability, Cullum and his team quickly turned Economic into an extremely attractive business with a market valuation some five times its 1993 purchase price. The journey was not without its casualties however and fifty percent of the original staff cadre had to go in the process. This was a deeply unpleasant and disturbing thing to have to do but major surgery was required if the body was to live. The management team had to work immensely hard to motivate the survivors. Cullum had been warned by Marek Gummieny of Candover that the remaining staff would not thank him for saving their jobs if in the process it made the MBO team millions. The reality in Economic was very different. Cullum ensured that staff received share equivalents so that they too would benefit from any eventual sale and profits made.

The majority of staff that remained were young and inexperienced but they worked tirelessly, weekends included, to clear out the poor performing risks and catch up with backlogs. Key distributors were 'loved to death' and a real partnership ethos evolved. Once the central crisis had passed Dyer realised that Economic had become FUN. There was a sense of frontiership about the place. Nothing stayed the same for long. The pace of change and progress was addictive.

The day after Peter Cullum returned to announce the management buy out, at a hastily arranged meeting set up to explain the future of the business, he was totally taken aback to be presented with a specially purchased Silver Tea Service as a token of thanks from all the Economic staff.

This gesture meant, and still means, a tremendous amount to him. Indeed his own words convey the feeling best: 'If I could only rescue one material thing from my burning house, it would be that Tea Service.'

There really were some dark and painful days inside Economic, it was a tremendous emotional roller-coaster, but it was eventually worthwhile for, and appreciated by, everyone involved in the journey.

Economic Insurance Company Limited December 1994

Managing Director's Review

Peter Cullum

"1994 has undoubtedly been a key year in the 93 year history of Economic Insurance, and it sets the scene perfectly for 1995 "

Momentum for Profitable Growth

In my report for the year ended 31 December 1993, I wrote of the work that all staff had undertaken to move the Company forward to a position of recording a pre tax profit of £4m for the year and the structural changes that led to the Management Buyout of December 1993. I characterised the Company's position at the end of 1993 as "perfectly placed to succeed".

I am glad to report that my forecast was accurate and the Financial Statements of the Company for the year ended 31 December 1994 show a

scheme business has been achieved in conjunction with our specialist intermediaries with whom we have developed new business plans playing to our mutual strengths.

1994 presented a number of opportunities to broaden the Company's base and two specific acquisitions have been made during the year. In September we announce the agreement to acquire Roy London General Broker Division, with its £10 commercial line business, co existi

new computer system. The transfer of data and the development of new software has required management to reallocate resources to solve individual problems. The new AS400 based system has in fact been introduced over only twelve a real acc

Cullum never forgot the manifest truth that the spirit and endurance of a business's staff, their attitude, is often as (or even more) important than their technical aptitudes. As Alan Sykes, the Chairman of Economic at the time of the MBO, reminded Cullum. 'The balance sheet goes home every Friday night and it is the CEO's job to ensure that they come back every Monday morning full of enthusiasm and endeavour!'

There was another, subtle, lesson to be learnt from the whole MBO sale process too.

At one stage it was possible that a well known (and

giant) corporation would buy the company. In financial terms this was a very attractive proposition, but the reality for the staff was likely to have been a bloodbath. This was not an option Cullum would contemplate. Loyalty had been a core mantra at the renewed Economic, and staff would not now be hung out to dry.

In July 1996 Economic was sold to Hiscox, a leading Lloyd's insurer. Another lesson was learned in the first few months of the new ownership, it was the critical and difficult nature of integration into a new culture. The management team learned the hard way that whatever the logic, and no matter what 'integration processes' (MI, Committees etc) are created, the truly vital component is the human dimension. People on both sides need to like each other, to be comfortable with each other and be seen to enjoy each other's company, and to commit to the same agreed plan with enthusiasm. It was a vital lesson that Cullum would use to good effect in his next incarnation.

Metamorphosis

The personal development journey that had begun with Cullum's decision to take on Economic was now accelerated by the successful MBO, the spectacular turn-around of the company and the subsequent sale to Hiscox. Each of these phases had involved intense negotiations, serious analysis and decision-making, periods of truly cliff-hanging suspense and occasions when the possibility of financial ruin was very real indeed. No-one comes through such experiences unaltered.

By the Autumn of 1996 Peter Cullum (whether he knew it or not) was on a trajectory that had only one logical destination: to bring about serious change in the UK Insurance market.

Following the sale of Economic to Hiscox, Thomas predicted that Cullum would last a maximum of eighteen months in the newly formed management structure. He was gone in less than twelve. The innate entrepreneurial drives that had (inevitably) been constrained or self-suppressed in his pre-Economic days were now up close and personal. There was absolutely no way he could be 'part of a machine' or simply the 'paid help' ever again, not even if it was an absolutely vital part of an absolutely superb machine. Cullum now needed to create his own machine.

The lessons learned at Economic simmered in Cullum's mind. Whatever his peers in the industry thought, for him there was revolutionary change in the air. Economic had proved that specialist intermediaries had real power which, used effectively, could provide real leverage – only the cooing of the key, profitable, agents of Economic had provided the platform for survival. How to harness that power for the future? On the day Cullum resigned from Hiscox, to formulate a business plan for a new vehicle of his imagination, the company that would eventually become "Towergate", Thomas asked Dyer (who has worked closer and longer with Cullum than anyone else) what he thought of it all.

Dyer sat back in his chair and considered the implications, then he let out a resigned sigh and made one of his trademark pithy observations:

'The man is incredible ... absolutely incredible ... and unquestionably mad ... God knows what's going to happen ... let's go to the pub.'

Within weeks Paul Dyer had begun writing up the business plan and was working with Cullum to finalise details. After the first month they were joined by Tony Proverbs, Sales Manager at Economic, who had left Hiscox and joined Cullum and Dyer in the business wilderness. Fun and games were back on the agenda!

Some Key Lessons Learned from the Economic Experience:
- To succeed in any truly challenging venture we need to question the validity of our fear thresholds. In our view fear thresholds are innately over-conservative. Their purpose, in the absence of any imminent threat to our well-being, is to maintain the status quo. This is fine if the status quo is what we want, but our true potential will not be realised if our fear thresholds are irrationally pessimistic. The decision of whether to take on a real challenge or to go for a more certain route will ultimately come down to gut-feelings. All truly challenging opportunities involve uncertainty, the absence of complete data, and no amount of conscious analysis will provide 'the right answer'. Psychological studies indicate that some eighty percent or

more of the processing that goes on in our brains occurs well below the consciousness threshold. Faced with making any important decision an effective strategy is to collect as much information as possible on the pros and cons of the various possibilities, think very hard about these possibilities for a relatively short period of time and then forget about them altogether. Your brain will not forget about them! Unconscious cognitive processes will continue to sift, compare, analyse, contrast and evaluate them. The result of this unconscious brain processing is sometimes experienced as an 'Ah-Ha' moment, the sort of thing that happens when the answer to a perplexing problem (such as suddenly remembering the name of some long-forgotten obscure actor or weird book that hours of conscious deliberation had previously failed to generate) just seems to 'jump into our heads' when we least expect it. Alternatively this unconscious brain processing may manifest itself as a 'gut feeling' telling us that we should or should not move in a particular direction.

Our advice is to listen carefully to it!

- Prior to the Economic MBO no-one involved in the buy-out process had any real expertise of 'serious' financial dealings. We were, like most, somewhat in awe of what we assumed to be an arcane and deeply cerebral art, the sort of activity from which mere mortals such as ourselves would be eternally excluded. Nothing could have been further from the truth. Planet Finance, just like everything else in fact, turned out to be populated with human beings who had no more and no fewer strengths or limitations than we ourselves had. We met a few incredibly bright people and others who were clearly not the fastest ants on the hill. And the rules of serious finance turned out to be understandable too, mostly rational and rather predictable. The experience taught us that in reality there probably are no 'higher functions' out there, staffed by super-humans who only deign to mingle with mortals under extreme duress. Just like us, time and chance happeneth to them too!

- No action checklist or set of step-by-step 'Effective Negotiating' principles would have significantly helped us through the MBO process (Cullum has a marked preference for 'real life' business histories and biographies that combine theory with actual practice*.) We were, of course, the product of a good deal of management training and experience, but in the end we were down to common-sense, animal cunning and, above all else, sheer self-belief (as epitomised by Peter Cullum's propensity to enter all negotiations with the implicit attitude that the other side just needed to see how good our ideas were and they would be begging to throw money at us!)

Our negotiating strategy changed continuously as the circumstances changed, we would go from 'let's just survive until tomorrow' to 'let's win this totally now' in the space of thirty minutes. It taught us that the real world of business negotiating and deal-making is exponentially 'messier' than the stuff we often see in text books or analyse in academic case studies. As Dyer, who is renowned for his ability to insert a military analogy into any miniscule pause in conversation commented at the time;

> 'all battle plans disintegrate on first contact with the enemy' boy was he right!

We are not implying that the study of theories of management, negotiation, decision-making or any other of the plethora of 'management' topics available these days is a pointless activity. That would be something of an oxymoron in a book such as this! Rather we would invoke the

*E.g. 'Barbarians at the Gate', 'Liar's Poker.'

observation of the psychologist BF Skinner who famously commented that;

> *'Education is what remains when what has been learned has been forgotten.'*

That stated, it has to be acknowledged that a good proportion of managers seem totally unaltered by their involvement in 'management development' activities while others are prone to believe whatever theory or technique they have most recently been exposed to.

Yet others, often seduced by the fact that they hold impressive management qualifications, seem to view the business world as something akin to an algorithm with inputs, processes, outputs, rational-economic decision making and utility maximisations underlying all activities. Maybe they are partly correct, and in all probability we ourselves were influenced and guided (perhaps it was those unconscious brain processes again) by the complex theories and concepts we had been exposed to during our years of formal management education. But when push came to shove we relied heavily on gut feelings, quick thinking, a total focus on the here and now and a firm belief (based on the numbers and a clear business proposition) that we had something very worthwhile on the table.

Any notion that we went in armed with a step-by-step contingency-based negotiating plan would be a long way from the truth. It was much more 'hand-to-hand combat than smart-bombs', to paraphrase Dyer!

- Faced with testing and uncertain predicaments the overwhelming majority of human beings look for an effective leader to ... well ... lead. This need for effective leadership is instinctive and has probably been built into our genes through the numerous millennia of natural selection.

During the Economic MBO and turnaround and the subsequent establishment of Towergate, Thomas and Dyer saw Cullum provide effective leadership in spadefulls. Not just the 'first-to-work-last-to-leave-sixteen-hour-days' stuff, although he most certainly did that, but the sort of leadership that inspires people to keep pushing on even when the bad-luck-grenades go off right in the bunker. And although he constantly, and correctly, emphasises the point that 'Towergate is team sport' it would be illusory to deny the fact that Towergate would not exist if it were not for Cullum's leadership. He provided it day in and day out at Economic. He made very hard and sometimes extremely difficult personal decisions, he upset people, bullied people, charmed people, developed people, exasperated people with his endless requests for 'more', fired people up, fired people, persuaded Thomas to abandon a healthy client list and join in, gave Dyer industrial-strength dyspepsia and made almost everyone in the company laugh out loud at some point.

The perennial question of whether leaders such as Peter Cullum are 'born' or 'made' (more on that topic later) is one that Dyer and Thomas have pondered for some considerable time. The current prognosis is that he was manufactured by NASA.

CHAPTER 2

Transitions

*If you do not change direction, you may
end up where you are heading.*

Lao Tzu

What are businesses for?

The question above, unlike the one that opened this book, is rarely if ever asked.

When it is asked the answer seems pretty obvious to most people:

'… to make money of course'.

Yes, making money is a significant factor in the founding rationale of the majority of businesses. But is it the entire rationale? Or even the greater part of it?

If the answer to that question is 'yes' it implies that entrepreneurs set up businesses for the primary purpose of monetary gain. In some instances of course this may be true. Organisations, like most things, exist somewhere on a continuum. The business spectrum has the likes of open air market-traders (Trotter's Independent Trading) and the rip-off merchants we see exposed on undercover TV programmes at one end and organisations such as Fair Trade and Ethical Investment at the other.

Most businesses are positioned somewhere in-between (with the avowed intent of not consciously aspiring to the market-trader-Del-Boy end!)

At the very beginning of the Towergate journey Peter Cullum and his colleagues sought to spell out the core reasons why they were taking such a considerable leap into the unknown. The venture held substantial personal and financial risks for all concerned; this was not an MBO, this was the establishment of an entirely new organisation based on operating principles previously unheard of in the historically staid world of UK insurance. Also, given the highly innovative nature of the core business proposition (a radical re-engineering of who does what for what return) the probability of success was difficult to estimate with any real accuracy (although Cullum never accepted this). What was certain however was that terms such as 'weekend', 'holiday' and 'work-life balance' would be disappearing from the lexicon for the foreseeable future. Therefore, given the considerable personal challenges that lay ahead, it was crucial for the founding group to clarify the wider reasons (wider than financial considerations alone that is) for embarking on the journey.

First off, however, Cullum needed to convince everyone involved that the end-goal was actually achievable. Thomas, who was engaged in the start-up but not exposed to the range of personal risks carried by the founders, remembers the event as a turning point.

Cullum's sheer force of will and total confidence in the project were extremely difficult to run against. Accepting that there were indeed uncertainties involved he made the (logical) point that if success in this or any business venture was certain then everyone with half a brain would be doing it. But there was much more to his routine than the obligatory 'we can do it' motivational rant. The intensity of Cullum's personal belief was matched by a fluent use of numbers and a crystal-clear business rationale. As the underlying logic of the proposition sank in I began to wonder why no one else had seen this opportunity. Then it dawned on me that this is precisely how business visionaries function, they see the 'obvious' before everyone else does.

As an independent consultant I had sat through many similar presentations and watched numerous 'change agents' stand up and do the 'vision thing'. The overwhelming majority of these presentations had been highly engaging displays of enthusiasm and commitment, sincerely delivered to be sure, but basically hype – hype that usually fell over when clever people started asking the really hard questions.

What was different here was an intense commitment

and enthusiasm coupled with a demonstrable, numbers-driven business rationale that had a starting point, an on-going strategy and an end view. I had heard plenty of hype in my time, hype is necessary at the concept stage of any innovative venture, but hype is not a business plan. This was both.

Despite the passion and clarity of Cullum's ideas, the highly innovative nature of the proposition meant that the sector challenges involved would be considerable. He was heartened however by ex-Chairman Alan Sykes' assertion that the Economic team could manage something much bigger.

Towergate: An Industry Challenge.

Very early after the sale of their now-profitable Economic business it became clear to the senior management team that their sojourn within Hiscox would not be a lengthy one. The cultural and operating differences were simply too great. The process of buying Economic and managing it back to serious profitability had opened everyone's eyes to the possibilities of even greater innovation and change within the UK Insurance sector. Suddenly the marbled halls of the mighty no longer looked unassailable, on the contrary they seemed fallible.

It is important to recognise that *the* key lessons learned during the Economic journey were fundamental to the conception and foundation of Towergate. In many ways Economic was the key learning experience for everyone involved, hence the strong emphasis on it here. Economic made everyone aware of the possibilities for fundamental change within the UK insurance sector and Towergate is the physical manifestation of that awareness.

Challenging accepted wisdom had been Peter Cullum's

modus operandi for many years and the experience of achieving substantial commercial success (against considerable odds) at Economic further strengthened his resolve to make a difference and also expanded his perspective on what level of business change was actually possible. He began to formulate an operational plan that would challenge much of the accepted wisdom surrounding the post-war model of non-life insurance in the UK and generate win-win opportunities for everyone involved in the distribution channel.

Interestingly, the more that Hiscox managers focused their efforts on moulding Economic into a classic Lloyds and London Market machine, with its underwriting dominance, the more it focused Cullum's mind on the wider potential of the provincial (outside of London) market, and on one key factor in particular.

That factor underpins Cullum's much-repeated mantra that '*The keys to success in this business are Distribution, Distribution and Distribution.*' It doesn't matter how good an underwriter or manufacturer you are, if you can't get the product to the customer you are dead in the water.

The strategic decision to refocus Economic on Schemes, niche markets and first-class underwriting results had proved, despite the qualms of many industry pundits who counselled that broking and specialist underwriting were effectively dead, that the opposite was true. This fact, combined with some serendipitous demography, set Cullum and his colleagues on their journey.

The so-called 'baby boomer' bulge had not passed the insurance sector by and in the mid 1990's many non-life underwriting agencies were managed by individuals who were actively considering an exit from their businesses within the coming ten years. Cullum, Dyer and the Economic management team had forged strong relationships with many such individuals and now that the constraints of the London Market were left behind them there was a certain inevitability to the notion that the newly formed Towergate (1997) should consider acquiring some of their companies. This was a revolutionary concept at the time, acquisitions were virtually unheard of in the regional insurance broking market and no pricing model with any degree of flexibility existed. Big Broker consolidations had changed the shape of global players at the top end of the UK market but the bulk of distribution lay untouched. However, despite the 'newness' of the concept, Cullum's acquisition rationale was predicated on a number of historical facts:

- Underwriting agents (Managing General Agents in the US) were widely perceived as being little more than incidental 'sideshows' by most major insurers and had experienced limited profitability.

- No-one working inside a major insurer had made their careers by specialising in Scheme business underwritten by outsourced third party agents, and this was despite the clear evidence that some of these agents were essentially more effective underwriters than the insurers themselves! The systematic development of broker-based underwriting businesses had been largely ignored.

- The already opaque relationship which existed between insurer and underwriting agent was often exacerbated by a (seemingly purposeful) use of obscure language and data that was at best confusing and in some instances virtually meaningless to the underwriting agencies themselves.

- Despite the fact that underwriting agencies virtually 'owned' the end-customer base (in terms of personal data acquired, relationships created and distribution expertise developed) the insurer commonly occupied the 'psychological power position'. In reality all that the insurer brought to the party was the strength of their balance sheet. This 'master-slave' relationship had been established after the second world war and had remained virtually unchallenged since that time. Cullum was determined to change it.

- Many insurers appeared less and less interested in marketing and distribution as their boards became increasingly dominated by executives who believed that all risks could be assessed through historical data evaluation. In many ways the 'human interface' between insurance companies and their customers had become an obstacle to an ongoing quest for numerical perfection in risk analysis. Emergent events such as the pandemic terrorism threat, global warming, selective climate change, misunderstood technology, easy access to litigation, mass migration and substantial social change, by virtue of the fact that they were historically unprecedented, did not fit the model and were to all intents and purposes ignored. The logical end-game of this numbers-driven approach to risk assessment would be the development of intelligent underwriting software that would render significant human involvement unnecessary. In consequence many UK insurers 'let go' of large swathes of their employees - many of them past the mythical 'over-the-hill' age of 50 – in a purge that ranks as a strong contender for the award of 'most devastating destruction of shareholder assets in commercial history'.

- A number of insurers, often under pressure from their institutional shareholders, succumbed to the prevalent wisdom that 'bigger is better' and engaged in a range of ill-prepared mergers. This big-machine mentality further constrained their ability to innovate and get closer to their customer base – the game was focused on cost-savings and introspection.

Market Consolidation

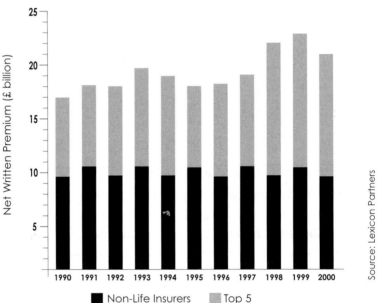

Source: Lexicon Partners

While all this was rattling around the marbled halls of the Leviathans, underwriting agents and insurance brokers got on with doing what they new best; de-risking the lives and businesses of their clients and providing them with a personal, human, service. This was the differential-value proposition that Cullum identified.

Consequently, with the modest funds provided by the sale of Economic and an intuitive belief in the power of marketing, excellent underwriting, good distribution and personal service, Cullum and Dyer were inexorably drawn to the conclusion that the next step on their journey of innovation would be to buy specialist underwriting agencies.

An easy decision to make in principle, considerably more difficult in execution. Which business should they go for? How would they fund the acquisitions? Would owners really sell?

Familiar territory seemed the obvious place to start looking and the criteria for selection was established quite early on. To be 'in the frame' for a possible acquisition a business needed to display the following:

- Sound underwriting results
- Good quality, experienced staff
- An owner who would remain in place for some time post-acquisition
- Clear control of distribution channels
- Control of customer 'ownership' and data

An underwriting agency that met these criteria (plus all necessary due diligence requirements) became a prime target for acquisition. One other key factor revealed itself over time – both Towergate management and the vendors had to get on well together and be able to establish an emotional bond.
Once acquired, Cullum and his team knew that they could drastically improve the financial performance of the business by:

- **leveraging underwriting results with improved terms**. Many insurers did not focus on the underwriting results of their intermediaries despite the fact that they were often worth millions! Leverage was never obtained at a cost to end-customers but through a more equitable renegotiation of the financial split between insurer and underwriting agency. After all the underwriting agency did virtually everything necessary to deliver the service, from attracting customers right through to handling their claims, thus the insurer's expense ratio consisted largely of fixed costs, a somewhat unpalatable truth that many found difficult to accept initially.

- **improving marketing**. Cullum and Dyer are out and out marketeers at heart and both recognised that although marketing efforts were sometimes satisfactory, often they were barely adequate. There were usually real opportunities for improvement, particularly through distribution.

- **strengthening the overall management function**. Most intermediaries had been traditional 'one man shows' - very successful within those historical constraints - but open to serious improvement. Many had no real business planning in place, no discernible growth strategy and quite often a lack of sophisticated financial expertise.

The rationale for acquisition and improvement was therefore in place, next the team needed to source the capital. The experience Cullum and Dyer had gained through the MBO process at Economic proved invaluable at this point. Although the new challenge was substantial and in many ways different from that at Economic, much of the mystique associated with the arcane world of high finance had been dispersed. Armed with a renewed enthusiasm and passion for the dream and (as ever) a bunch of numbers, projections, financial analyses, development plans and quite irrefutable logic, Cullum went hunting for capital. It may have been a 'blue-sky' prospect (as many potential investors insisted on terming it) but Cullum was eventually able to overcome the conservatism of the market.

By March 1998, only six months after completing the purchase of the first 'Towergate business' performance results made it clear that, if anything, Cullum had been over-cautious in his evaluation of the power of the new business model! The original targets seemed immensely stretching at the time: £100m Premium, £30 million income and £10 million profit, over a 5-year period. It had previously taken Economic more than eighty years to generate £60m premium!

The potential for further acquisitions now seemed enormous as Cullum's team, together with a very small cadre of initially sceptical insurers, came to a growing realisation that something quite special could be on the cards.

Towergate's head-count had by this point expanded to the giddy total of seven individuals. Tony Proverbs, who had been at Economic and Hiscox, was Sales Director while Ann Fulton, Teresa Davis, Lindsey Morgan and Peter Alexander, veterans of the Economic-Hiscox journey also, divided all other organisational functions between themselves. Everyone involved worked like lunatics, making the tea, filing the letters, attending to all the paraphernalia necessary to keep a fledgling business in some sense of order, and all carried out in what could at best be described as 'functional' premises. It could be kindly described as 'functional' premises but it was in fact a building in need of some considerable refurbishment, as exemplified by the occasion on which Dyer was summoned to remove a dead rat which had contrived to expire in the 'lobby!'

It needs to be stressed at this stage that all successful business ventures (successful ventures of all types for that matter) can appear somewhat inevitable when viewed through the comforting rear-mirror of hindsight. This is absolutely not the case in real-time however! The entrepreneurial journey is fraught with uncertainty, disappointment, fear, joy, unbearable tension, excitement and, most terrifying of all, a day-to-day awareness that some unanticipated 'event' could easily scupper everything. Nothing is ever one hundred

Professional Broking November 1997

Peter Cullum, Paul Dyer (seated) and Tony Proverbs

Tower of strength

"It is no surprise that Peter Cullum and Paul Dyer's new venture is scheme-based. But Tim Collinson says that its federal structure breaks new ground"

"In effect we are a virtual insurance company, doing all the elements of a normal company but not carrying the risks – we don't want sleepless nights about equity markets and solvency margins."

percent certain. No matter how good the plan or how charismatic the leader, the business sea can change in an instant and a fledgling corporate vessel can be done for. It requires a certain type of 'front-of-mind' optimism combined with a 'back-of-mind' realism to succeed. Optimism alone is simply not enough and blind optimism can be positively lethal. Everyone involved in the start-up of Towergate knew the very real risks inherent in the venture they were undertaking and each dealt with them in their own particular ways.

As Dyer recalls:

"There are moments when you wake up sweating, knowing the risks you run, both financially and emotionally, but you also know that you only get one shot at life. When you see the possibility of achieving something quite special you require either a very strong or a very dull will not to be tempted!"

The success of the initial Towergate venture meant that horizons expanded rapidly and it became increasingly clear that substantial finance would be required to capitalise on momentum. Now the serious money-men would need to be involved!

Dyer's reflections on this quest for funding are illuminating:

"In many ways investment bankers are a sort of 'priesthood' who admit the uninitiated novice into their temples only under considerable duress. Displaced from the actual front-line of entrepreneurial battle they often play psychological power-games with those obliged to seek assistance in obtaining the ordnance (capital) necessary to move forward. Early in any relationship communications are characteristically formal with a liberal abundance of obscure insider jargon peppering almost every discussion. Whether this is intended to 'intimidate the peasants' is open to question but you certainly get the feeling that some pleasure is gained from the inevitable confusion it engenders in the uninitiated. However, deep within the corporate shell there often lurks a slowly beating human heart and it is refreshing to see that 'a dream', especially when it is conveyed by someone as passionate and convincing as Peter Cullum, can get that moribund heart racing a little. Well for a while at least!"

Towergate's original bankers, Royal Bank of Scotland, did eventually become emotionally involved in the venture although there did exist (in the early days at least) a real struggle to define 'who needed who most.' Cullum was absolutely certain what the answer to that question was! It is to the Royal Bank of Scotland's credit that they bought into the idea early on and had enough vision to push for a controlling equity stake, firmly reputed by Cullum. Whatever the pain, whatever the panics, whatever the lack of liquidity, Cullum never faltered in the unshakeable belief that it would all turn out fine.

The third group to become emotionally involved in the Towergate dream were the insurers themselves, but it was certainly not a case of love at first sight!

Cullum's mantra that success in the insurance sector was about 'distribution, distribution and distribution' did not hang easily with them. An historical focus on product orientation and a belief in the inherent superiority of in-house underwriting over tawdry distribution by insurance brokers was, for insurers at least, a self-evident truth chiselled in granite for all time. Peter Cullum begged to differ.

From Cullum's perspective insurers had for years stubbornly refused to countenance the possibility (the fact in his view) that profits from scheme businesses run by external agencies were, in some respects, propping up disastrously poor in-house underwriting results. These agencies, often generating a fifty percent better return than conventional distribution methods, were in fact subsidising a grossly ineffective system whereby preferential relationships were forged not on the basis of exceptional underwriting performance but often through simple position in a historically established social hierarchy. Despite the considerable evidence from Retailing and Manufacturing that distribution was key, underwriters (especially in Lloyds) still sat waiting patiently for business to be bought to them by penitential Brokers. The Revolution was at hand.

Armed with the financial facts (as ever) Cullum took the underwriting results (profits) from his soon-to-be-acquired agencies to insurers and stated flatly that he was not prepared to subsidise substandard in-house underwriting performance by accepting a ludicrously unfair return on the considerable profits his businesses would be generating for them. It has to be remembered that Cullum's businesses would be expected to carry all the operating expenses (apart from reinsurance costs) themselves. The insurer's own expenses were consequently largely their fixed costs. It simply wasn't equitable. The time had come, as they say, for many insurers to 'get real.'

Fortunately some were more than happy to consider the sorts of Return on Premium figures that Cullum's newly re-engineered businesses promised to deliver. Cullum was indeed able to outperform their in-house underwriting.

Change, fundamental change, is rarely easy to contemplate or accept. The UK insurance sector had trundled through the nineteen-seventies, eighties and early nineties largely undisturbed by the seismic upheavals that were fundamentally reshaping sectors such power generation, transport, manufacturing, retailing and consumer electronics. By the end of the 1990's however, the penalty had been paid. Underwriting performance in the UK had collapsed.

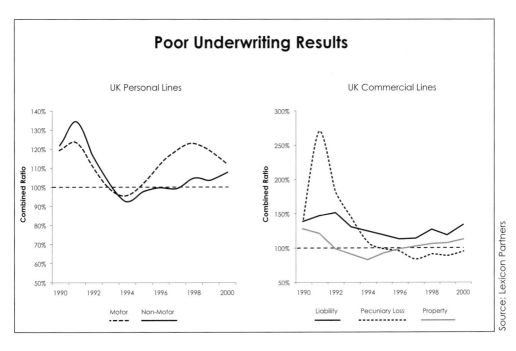

Expenses had risen significantly and by the end of the decade £23 billion of stakeholder value had been destroyed along with the near-destruction of Lloyds.

Critically, a major shift had occurred in distribution.

Value Destruction
in the 1990's

£23 billion

(before investment income)

Source: Lexicon Partners

Huge Marketing budgets were allocated to Direct Marketing and most strategic planners were convinced that Insurers could control all distribution.

Sooner or later it is inevitable that the 'Barbarians' of change will come banging at the gates. It is to the credit of those Insurance Company Directors who saw the necessity for change that they reached out, somewhat reluctantly at first, and then actively embraced what was essentially a 'win-win' opportunity for all involved.

Back on the Farm

Of course simply drawing up a devastating battle-plan and acquiring the necessary munitions to charge ahead are not synonymous with winning the war! The map is not the territory. With a growing realisation that Towergate could be a much bigger beast than anyone had initially contemplated, the founding group needed to establish some clear operating principles.

A central point made by Cullum was that no-one at Towergate should be opposed to making money! This maxim was established at the very beginning. There would be no apologies for being good at what we did, reinventing and reengineering business processes, adding value to a wide range of stakeholders, maximising revenue and ploughing it back into an aggressive business expansion and acquisition programme. The P&L account would be, and remains, the literal bottom line at Towergate, but the P&L account would not be the end of the story. Everyone involved understood that making money would be a necessary but not sufficient condition for driving the business forward. There needed to be something more.

The motivational theorist Frederick Herzberg famously claimed that money is not in truth a work motivator but merely a 'hygiene factor' something that demotivates when it is felt to be inadequate but produces little lasting motivation when an acceptable level of remuneration has been achieved. Doubling an individual's salary for example will not necessarily double that person's resolve and commitment to the organization, but halving it will produce substantial results in the opposite direction! Fred appears to have got it right. Salaries, commissions and bonuses have incredible potency in the realm of motivation-reduction but precious little to offer in terms of *sustainable* spirit-lifting.

And it is no different at corporate level. For Towergate's senior management, financial results are an *indicator* of the overall health of the business, a proxy variable that shows whether the company is doing more things right than wrong.

Financial results are the consequence of a myriad of underlying activities. They include an organisation's own sales efforts, competitor's sales efforts, internal training, product development, product placing, marketing, competitor moves, internal cost control, internal recruitment policies, changes in statutory requirements, incentives, teamwork, product offerings, changing customer preferences …these and many other factors will impact on the all-important, all-revealing bottom line. But, important as they are, bottom line financial results can turn toxic if they are allowed to become ends in themselves. When financial results do become ends in themselves people can be tempted to find methods of achieving them that are not conducive to the long-term health of the business: witness rogue trader Nick Leeson and the destruction of his employer, UK Merchant Bank Barings!

To remain truly healthy, businesses need to define a set of core non-financial operating principles that link with and support their financial goals.

So what were Towergate's non-financial operating principles to be? The immediate answer to that question was firmly centred on people. But first the group needed to face up to some practicalities.

'Our people are our greatest asset' is one of those business mantras that is repeated so often it has become virtually meaningless in operational terms. Every corporate report contains the adage in some shape or form. And although Cullum and his colleagues believed the statement to be true, they needed to find a way of expressing it that would convey the message credibly and at the same time provide practical operational guidelines. First they tackled the credibility issue.

Motivation is one of the key ingredients in any success recipe, be it personal or organisational, business or non-business. Everyone understands that. If business A and business B operate in similar markets with similar product offerings and have similar skill-sets and technologies (which is certainly true of the financial services sector) then the motivation levels of their respective employees will provide one of (if not **the**) key differentiating factors determining their relative success. Therefore, to use contemporary business-speak, how could Towergate achieve staff 'buy-in' and enhance its chances of success?

Gaining Staff Commitment

Organisations have often resorted to well-trodden paths in their search for the fabled city of 'empowered and committed staff'. One such path involves earnest exhortations of 'teamwork' 'self-belief' 'excellence' 'customer-focused quality' 'market leadership' and 'pride'. Such exhortations are often found on the corporate pens, kitchenware and expensively framed 'motivational' photographs that adorn the corridors of many organisations.

The question of course is, do they work? Thomas has a personal view:

'Motivational' messages need to be backed up with appropriate actions. You're far better off saying nothing than saying something that you don't follow up on or, much worse, clearly act against. The best of your people will be acutely aware of any inane

motivational gimmicks or message/action discrepancies. Many senior managers would be mortified if they knew the true level of cynicism such gimmicks and actions commonly engender in their most able staff.

Say something motivational only when you truly mean it, and make sure you act in accordance with your message. And as far as gimmicks are concerned experience suggests a general rule of thumb: every trite 'motivational slogan' increases cynicism by 5%, and every puerile 'let's be the best' poster, pen and mug campaign increases it by 10%.

The principal driver underpinning Towergate's success has been a continuous desire for innovation and change among the key players 'reinvention every three years' is a common

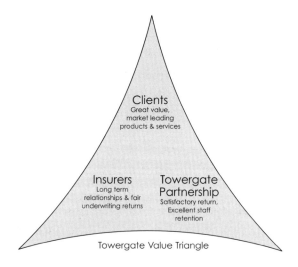

Towergate Value Triangle

Cullum dictate. Nothing stays the same for long. The business acquisition rate has been phenomenal. In response Towergate staff have sometimes railed at yet another new company purchase, yet another systems integration, yet another product rationalisation and cried 'enough for now'. Then they have stepped up a gear. Some have almost buckled at times of intense pressure, some have removed themselves from the eye of the storm and others have been removed from it. Cullum often uses a 'bus' analogy: at first people are invited to get on board for the 'Towergate journey', second they are given the opportunity to disembark if they discover that they are not happy with the route, the driving or the destination, as a last resort malcontents who do not voluntarily disembark may be evicted. Most often however we have seen people accomplish things they did not believe or even know they were capable of. Account handlers have become Managing Directors of sizeable Towergate businesses in fewer than five years.

The key driver for Towergate's senior executives is intellectual rather than financial, it is really about innovation and problem-solving:

Where's the gap no-one has noticed?
Where can the finances be re-engineered?
Where's the gross underperformance?
How many assumptions can we challenge?
How can we make this new idea work?

One of the major lessons we have learned from the Towergate experience to date is that to be successful, businesses need to create and sustain a palpable sense of urgency and challenge. Motivational slogans and framed prints of soaring Eagles or intrepid mountaineers don't really cut the mustard. Without an on-going sense of purpose and energy things stagnate. Personal and organisational comfort zones are not stable entities and contrary to the oft-quoted adage of Mr Parkinson that 'work expands to fill the time available for its completion' our experience is that left unchallenged, personal and organisational comfort zones contract and carry self-limiting notions of what constitutes 'work' and 'opportunity' along with them. Work doesn't really expand when a business loses its momentum, people's horizons shrink.

'Make Money. Have Fun. Do Good.'

This statement encapsulates Towergate's core operating principles. And in that order. Towergate is not a 'not-for-profit' organisation, it's very much for it! People are expected to work hard and bring home the bacon. But profit isn't everything and our core operating principles recognise the fact that people at all levels within a business are motivated by more than money alone (and no, we don't have it emblazoned on pens, mugs or posters) we make people aware of it when they join us and then we let our actions talk.

Towergate celebrates its 5th Anniversary
Left to right: Lindsey Morgan, Ann Fulton, Peter Cullum,
Tony Proverbs, Teresa Davis.

So to answer the question that opened this section: '*What are businesses for?*' our response would be: '***To provide an opportunity for people to work hard, develop personally and make money, to have fun and to do some good.***'

What do successful businesses do?

Depending on your particular intellectual bent there is an infinite number of possible answers to this question. Over the past fifty years or so literally thousands of books have been published, and indeed continue to be published, on the subject of 'How to run a successful company.'

Essentially these books all say (the same) two things:

'***Excite your people***' and '***Delight your customers***'.

The central difficulty of course is that a business may do both of these things extremely well and yet still go south. Take the much-quoted catechism that business success lies in *Delighting the customer*.

Consider this; if you or I were to set up a business tomorrow that offered top-brand lap-top computers (or anything else for that matter) at fifty percent of the manufacturer's production costs, we would do more than delight our customers we would positively electrify them with joy – for the brief period of time it took us to go from start-up to screw-up. Similarly with the sage advice to *Excite your people*.

Doubling salaries and halving workloads would probably achieve that aim nicely!

These comments are somewhat tongue-in-cheek we accept, but a good deal of truth and caution can be gained from thinking about them. Delighting our customers and exciting our people cannot be ends in themselves as far as any functional business is concerned because they are not the ultimate *outcomes* we seek. If they were then we could logically justify taking the sort of actions described above. Achieving customer satisfaction (or 'delight' or 'loyalty' or whatever the current buzz-phrase may be) and motivating our staff are simply two *inputs* that will impact on the ultimate *outcomes* businesses seek.

Confusing inputs with outcomes can nullify the extremely important question - *why*?

Why should a business delight its customers?

Why should a business excite its people?

These questions can clarify a crucial business distinction; the difference between inputs and outcomes.

Inputs and Outcomes

At Towergate there is a strong preference for *doing* as opposed to *theorising* and people are acutely aware of the dangers of the 'Knowing-Doing Gap' (see later.)

Peter Cullum has a caustic quip for individuals and groups who drift toward the 'analysis-to-paralysis' approach to problem solving and it encapsulates the prevalent attitude:

'Shall we make a decision or shall we talk about it for another two years!'

This is an important point. Whilst Cullum is absolutely committed to thorough analysis he is scathing of the sort of analysis that leads to 'reports' which describe in painstaking detail all the pluses and minuses of options A to Z but offer no opinion on action. It is the fear of getting things wrong, in his view, that leads to such inertia and is what holds most individuals and businesses back. 'Rational bravery', an ability to make a firm decision based on the available data and that ever-elusive 'feel' for a situation is a much-admired quality.

Another *cause celebre* of his stresses the need for businesses to continually strive for improvement, even when current performance is deemed to be more than satisfactory.

'You don't have to be ill to get better' is a 'Cullumism' well known to Towergate staff!

We believe that a good deal of business theorising is unnecessarily complex and that it is possible to speak simply about key business challenges without being ruinously simplistic in the process. To this end we have developed an operating model we call '*The Four Outcomes*' which is presented to newly recruited Towergate staff via the 'Towergate Foundation Day'. The model explains the core cultural and operating principles of the business.

Before we proceed however it may be useful to undertake the exercise we ask our new people to complete when they begin the session.

The exercise asks people to consider the following question:

> '*What are the **key** things that every organisation operating in a competitive environment **must** do in order to remain in business long-term?*'

Limit you answer to a maximum of six brief suggestions.

It may be worthwhile spending ten minutes or so on this exercise before you read on.

The six most common responses we receive at Towergate (in no particular order) are:

Recruit good people.
Develop excellent products.
Train your staff well.
Provide excellent customer service.
Pay your staff well.
Get your prices right.

These are rational responses and the majority of successful businesses will be likely to incorporate some if not all of them in their operating strategies.

But again they are essentially *inputs* rather than *outcomes* and again they beg the *why*? Question.

Why should we recruit good people?
Why should we train and pay them well?
Why should we provide excellent customer service?

These are not facetious questions. As we noted earlier, businesses may do many 'good' things yet still go down the pan. Conversely others may not adhere to 'good' practices at all yet mange to endure long term.

The bare fact is that inputs do not guarantee success and an overemphasis on getting inputs right may obscure the fact that they are there for a purpose, and that purpose is to generate desired *outcomes*.

So what should these business outcomes be?

We believe there are essentially four of them.

The Four Outcomes Approach

We believe that in order to survive long-term, businesses that operate in a competitive environment need to be exceptionally good at doing the following four things:

- *Retaining their existing profitable customers*
- *Growing their business with these customers and/or attracting new ones*
- *Reducing (ideally eliminating) unnecessary costs*
- *Keeping abreast (ideally ahead) of emerging developments in their marketplace*

Consider a company that is highly accomplished at achieving all Four Outcomes. People within the organisation know who the most profitable customers are (you'd be surprised at the number of businesses that simply don't) and they are exceptionally good at holding on to them.

And because they are good at holding on to them they have the opportunity to offer additional services and products to them over the long-term.

And because customers stay long-term it's easier to get referrals from them and enhance 'word-of-mouth' reputation.

Also, because people in the business are good at limiting unnecessary costs (not penny-pinching, just cutting the waste) they have a healthier bottom-line.

And because they have a healthier bottom-line they can invest in the research and development that gives them the best chance of staying abreast or ahead of crucial market and customer changes.

The Four Outcomes are a somewhat tautological definition of what long-term successful businesses *are* in that they describe what long-term successful businesses need to *do*. Such businesses (as long as they keep their focus firmly on these essentials) are, almost by definition, going to make it.

The first two outcomes, retaining existing profitable customers and attracting new ones, is acutely important for the insurance industry. Insurance is one of the few business sectors (another is gambling!) which accepts that it will inevitably attract a percentage customers who will not be profitable in the strict monetary sense – the losses of the few are paid for by the premiums of the many. These customers will receive a good deal more in legitimate claims payments than they will ever lay out in premiums. Indeed it is essentially the job of effective underwriters to ensure that potentially ruinous customers are kept out of the portfolio!

That said, there is often a strong temptation within the industry (very evident in the early days of Economic) to equate a healthy Gross Written Premium (the sum of premium sales) with a healthy business. GWP is a necessary but not sufficient condition for long-term success however and apart from the blunt indications of the loss ratio there are often considerable differences between the underlying costs of servicing various clients. At Towergate we have frequently been surprised by the results of rigorous cost-benefit studies which have shown that many low or mid-range GWP clients are actually more profitable pound-for-pound than those at the top of the list. High GWP usually equates to high visibility and high visibility usually equates to preferential treatment in terms of customer service and speed of response. While there is nothing wrong with this approach, and much to commend it, it can on occasions blind us to the fact that we may be missing opportunities to cement relationships with less visible clients who, collectively, may be equally or even more valuable over the long term.

The Four Outcomes approach has certainly helped us remain focused on the essentials of running a successful business. However, we are under no illusions that it is a guaranteed blueprint for success. Far from it. That of course depends upon…

People

Many people work hard. By this we mean that many people get to work on time or earlier, are busy for most of the working day, often leave later than their job descriptions require and are rarely if ever AWOL. They never take 'sickies', if they say they are unwell they really are unwell. A proportion of such people constitute the essential drivers of any company. These are the people who will keep the Business in business long-term and they can be found at all levels within an organisation.

But it is our clear assertion that only a *proportion* of the total workforce (including the hard-working ones) actually keep a company going long-term. And if that assertion holds water, what does it imply about the rest?

The People Spectrum

The philosopher Robert Zend once commented that *'people have one thing in common ... they are all different.'* We think he got that just about right!

Edgar Schein's notion of 'complex man' has influenced Peter Cullum's approach to management for many years.

People, as we have already noted, really are at the heart of any business success (or failure for that matter) and people, like everything else, tend to be positioned somewhere on a spectrum. At Towergate we see this spectrum as having 'Committed' at one end and 'Compliant' at the other. As far as business impact goes there is a huge difference between having a Committed as opposed to a Compliant work force.

People who are positioned well toward the 'Committed' end of the spectrum tend to 'live and breathe' the company. They give one-hundred and ten percent effort virtually one-hundred percent of the time. They may vary dramatically in terms of their actual impact on the company's long-term future, but their commitment is second to none. They fall into two types: *'Leaders'* and *'Troopers.'*

'Leaders' represent the driving force for the whole business. They are committed, capable and ambitious. Essentially they are 'Organisational Evangelists' who really do walk the talk and they can be found at all levels. As we will see later, these people are essential to winning 'hearts and minds' and their numbers are important. To prosper long-term it is our belief that an organisation must have between eight and twelve percent of its people, at all levels, who clearly display 'leader' qualities.

Next at the 'Committed' end of the spectrum we have *'Troopers.'*

'Troopers' are essential to any business. These are the

people who are happy to come to work and do their jobs well and then go home and live their lives. They often make a clear distinction between work and home life and are usually not 'ambitious' in the classic sense of the word.

As we shift toward the other end of the spectrum, the 'Compliant' pole, we commonly discover two very different types of individual: the '*In-house Retired*' and the '*Organisational Cynics*'.

The '*In-house retired*' are in some ways similar to '*Troopers*'. They too are reasonably happy to come to work, it's just that they aren't keen to actually do much of it when they get there. Such people have three million explanations why things don't get done and a further six million reasons why it wasn't their fault. A fair number of managers (too many probably) sideline these people after a while and then more or less ignore them. The trouble with this approach of course is that *somebody* has to do what the In-house retired should be doing (a Trooper usually) and that somebody, unsurprisingly, gets somewhat fed up about it.

Our view is that managers have a professional responsibility to either performance-manage the In-house retired back into the organisation's contributing workforce (which definitely can be done as we have so often seen at Towergate) or to performance-manage them out of it altogether.

Lastly there are the '*Organisational cynics*'. These people are dangerous. They either have a congenital propensity toward negativity or have been made that way by their experiences (often it's a combination of both). They are often quite intelligent - at least intelligent enough to manipulate themselves through the organisation's selection and promotion procedures and to remain in employment - but once safely ensconced within a company they usually begin a subversive campaign of nay-saying anything and everything that the business takes pride in.

'The share scheme here isn't as good as it is in ABC Co.'
'Our senior management hasn't got a clue what it's doing.'
'The company motto is bullshit, they don't care about anything but profit.'
'This new project is never going to work, it failed in ABC Co years ago.'

The majority of organizational cynics are shrewd enough to keep their views to themselves when in the company of people more senior, and in the presence of top management they often present themselves as 'martyrs-in-waiting', simply longing to die for the company cause. Watch out for them!

The Organisational 'Iceberg'

Every organisation resembles an iceberg

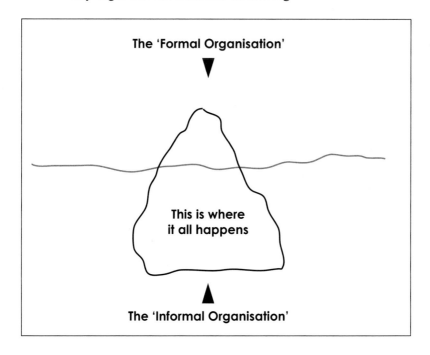

The 'Formal Organisation'

This is where it all happens

The 'Informal Organisation'

The part we see above the water-line is the 'Official Organisation', this is the public face of the business, the image presented in every corporate report. It includes avowed statements on worthy topics such as quality, responsibility, ethics, equality of opportunity, attitude to staff (*'Our greatest asset...'*) attitude to customers (*'We aim to delight our customers...'*) and so on.

It is not uncommon for a proportion of staff to scoff at these statements (and not just the Organisational Cynics who scoff at anything positive) because they feel that they experience a different set of values in the 'real' workplace, i.e. the 'Unofficial Organisation', from those espoused in the 'Official' one. This can occur for a number of reasons.

Not every supervisor or manager will embrace the values the organisation aspires to instil (indeed some may be Organisational Cynics themselves) and staff who work for these supervisors and managers will be at the receiving end of that discrepancy. In other instances of course the espoused values of the organisation may indeed be seen to be little more than 'image marketing' or just hype if there is a perceived lack of real commitment to the implementation of values.

Our experience strongly suggests that organisations must be very careful in this area and that the cardinal sin of *'over-promising and under-delivering'* is extremely pertinent here. That said however, it is probably impossible to please all of the people all of the time. No matter how hard an organisation believes in and strives to live up to its espoused values there will almost inevitably be a proportion of people who will, for a multitude of reasons both personal and non-personal, refuse to see the organisation as anything other than an evil empire!

The battle for the 'hearts and minds' of people is waged in the Unofficial Organisation and not the Official one. The Unofficial Organisation is where it really happens.

Rumour networks, disinformation, unauthorised practices, ad-hoc interest networks, unofficial 'opinion-shapers', heroes and villains, they are all there. The struggle to establish the dominant operational culture (are we working for the good guys or the bad guys?) is mainly fought between the Organisational Cynics and the Organisational Evangelists. And it is a battle that never ends.

When a business is performing well and there are opportunities for advancement, training, bonuses etc. the Organisational Cynics have a hard time of it. When things are going less well the Organisational Evangelists find the going rougher.

The unfortunate reality is that the Official Organisation's overt motivational efforts will inevitably pale in comparison to the power of covert messages generated within the Unofficial Organisation. It is here that actual day-to-day operating values will be forged. When there is a substantial degree of synchronicity between higher management's proclamations and 'word on the street' then almost anything is possible. When there is little or no synchronicity there will simply be lip-service and privately expressed derision and dissent. Businesses need to ensure that there are sufficient 'leaders' (and this is particularly true in terms of first-line supervisors and managers) present within the Unofficial Organisation to challenge the seemingly spontaneous tide of negativity which arises in the absence of any viable alternatives.

In the brief sections that follow we will examine some of the key factors which seem to characterise these crucially important organisational 'leaders'.

Choices, choices

Depending on your job description, you will have a degree of choice over the things you do at work in the coming weeks and months. If you are a front-line member of staff in an in-bound call-centre then the amount of choice you have will probably be limited. Maybe you will be able to switch shifts with a colleague or take some short-notice leave but other than that your opportunities for self-determination at work will probably be quite constricted. If you are the chief executive however you will have almost total control over what you choose to do (and how you do it) in the coming weeks.

Each situation has advantages and disadvantages for both people and organisations.

Choice is a double-edged sword. Too much of it can be overwhelming, too little can be soul-sapping. As we ascend the corporate 'ladder' the amount of choice available to us, and required of us, commonly increases. As we move upward we will be expected to make decisions about many things. How best to achieve the broad objectives set for us, where to spend our budget, what to do about problem person 'x', whether to allow person 'y' to take unexpected leave, who to appoint to a critical new position and so on. In many respects our competence will be judged on how well we make such decisions, so quite a lot rests on them.

People who have restricted choice at work also have fewer decisions to make (and consequently fewer opportunities to get them wrong). Front-line staff at an in-bound call centre know exactly what is expected of them; answer the telephone quickly and politely, resolve the customer's query wherever possible and escalate any others up the chain of command. It is an extremely important business function of course but only one real decision is required: can I resolve this call or do I need to pass it up the line? As a consequence it is highly unlikely that staff in such positions go home of an evening agonising about the decisions they have made during the previous eight hours.

Things are quite different as we move up the organisational ladder. People with 'management' responsibility (from first-line supervisor to CEO) often make significant decisions on a daily basis and they also have considerable flexibility in choosing what to focus their efforts on. This is an important point. In our opinion the most significant factors influencing both personal and organisational effectiveness are grounded in the ways in which key individuals respond to the basic question: 'what should I do next?'

This brings us right back to the statement made earlier in this chapter that businesses are driven forward by a relatively small number of people. These are the people who do the things that really matter long-term, the things that truly 'add value' as the jargon goes. When they decide what to do next they usually make the right choices.

Busy-busy

'*If you want something done, give it to a busy person.*' This cliché is pretty ubiquitous and there is probably some truth in it. Busy people are ... well ... *busy*. They are always active, rushing around with wads of paper in one hand and 'coffee-on-the-go' in the other. Such people have tremendous amounts of drive and they usually do get a lot of things done. The question we must ask of course is whether they tend to get the *right* things done. If they do, they are priceless, unfortunately this is not always the case. This is not to deride 'busy people' in any way, far from it, every organisation needs them. But drive alone, drive without *focus*, is not enough to ensure long-term personal or business success. A good number of individuals and organisations work extremely hard yet under-achieve because they do not focus their energies on the areas most important to their goals. There are a number of common reasons for this relative lack of achievement and we will consider a few of the most pernicious below.

The FT Effect

Every colleague we have worked with through the Towergate Academy Management Development Programme, without exception, has faced exactly the same challenge: they are extremely time-pressured. And they are not exaggerating.

Towergate is not an environment conducive to navel-gazing or philosophising. People work very hard indeed. Yet despite this common fact some people consistently achieve more than others. Why should that be?

There are various factors involved of course but the two key differentiating characteristics that appear most often in highly productive individuals are *focus* and *time utilisation*, what we call the FT effect.

Focus

Successful organisations and individuals are highly focused. They know what the most important factors influencing success are and they hone in on them like laser-guided bombs. As discussed above, people have various degrees of choice over the things they can focus their efforts on. Some individuals and organisations seem to make the most productive decisions consistently while others do not.

Clear goals are important in helping achieve focus (see next section) but they need to adapt to changing circumstances. At the inception of Towergate for example the generally accepted goal was to purchase maybe five or ten underwriting agencies in the first few years or so. Not long into the journey Peter Cullum was purchasing three a month!

The key to achievement is to concentrate efforts on the activities that are most likely to move us in the direction we seek to go. Cullum uses a straightforward three-stage process for clarifying organisational goals and prioritising actions that asks:

Where are we now?
Where do we want to get to?
How do we get from here to there?

Yes, it's simple, but it's certainly not simplistic, and woe betide anyone who injects any waffle, unsubstantiated assertions or bullshit into the deliberations!

Within the Towergate Academy we use a straightforward prioritisation tool, the **M-S-C** technique, to help our staff focus on the most important activities they need to undertake. The acronym stands for:

- **MUST do**
- **SHOULD do**
- **COULD do**

Must do activities, by definition, take priority over all others. Must do activities have non-negotiable deadlines and serious consequences for non-compliance. Tax returns, insurance renewals and crucial board reports for the CEO are a few examples.

When Towergate staff are introduced to this technique and asked to prioritise their current workloads using the M-S-C criteria, a very common lament is:

'Everything I have on my list is a Must do!'

This often has some substance to it but there is usually an element of self-infliction involved in the predicament! The vast majority of people's Must do's are not actually the result of unforeseen emergencies (such as having to react quickly to some catastrophe) but have in fact moved inexorably through the ranks of once being Could do's, and then Should do's, until (inevitably) they end up being Must do's!

The slippery slope usually begins at the 'Could do /Should do' stage. For reasons unknown to humanity an awful lot of people choose to focus on Could do's (and there are an infinite number of them of course) or even worse 'Shouldn't do's' when in fact they have clear Should do's staring them in the face. The consequence being that these Should do's inevitably mutate into the plethora of Must do's people so bitterly complain about!

Clarity about which activities are the most important to focus on at any given time, combined with a determination not to be distracted from them, constitute the bedrock of personal and organisational success. The M-S-C technique is a simple yet effective procedure that can help facilitate this.

Time Utilisation

The pace of work at Towergate is pretty frantic. And it's no different from the majority of successful organisations that are faced with stiff competition for customers and committed to a 'lean' operating philosophy. In general terms people within Towergate either develop effective coping strategies or they wilt.

A central skill, in addition to having clear priorities, is to be absolutely ruthless about minimising (ideally eliminating) time-wasting activities. Essentially there are four types of activity that people engage in at work. Each can be described in terms of a Proactive-Reactive and High Value-Low Value set of axes. In the Towergate Academy development programme we use the following matrix to help staff clarify the differences between them:

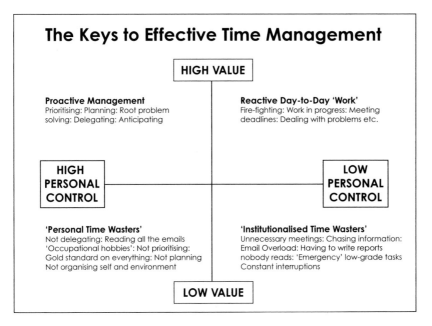

The Keys to Effective Time Management

HIGH VALUE

Proactive Management
Prioritising: Planning: Root problem
solving: Delegating: Anticipating

Reactive Day-to-Day 'Work'
Fire-fighting: Work in progress: Meeting
deadlines: Dealing with problems etc.

HIGH PERSONAL CONTROL

LOW PERSONAL CONTROL

'Personal Time Wasters'
Not delegating: Reading all the emails
'Occupational hobbies': Not prioritising:
Gold standard on everything: Not planning
Not organising self and environment

'Institutionalised Time Wasters'
Unnecessary meetings: Chasing information:
Email Overload: Having to write reports
nobody reads: 'Emergency' low-grade tasks
Constant interruptions

LOW VALUE

- Quadrant 1 Activities (Reactive – High Value) These activities constitute the majority of what could be described as 'day-to-day work'. They include such things as dealing effectively with customer queries, managing unforeseen difficulties, meeting deadlines, attending productive meetings, responding to directives from higher management and so on.

- Quadrant 2 Activities (Reactive – Low Value) These are activities that are often proscribed by the organisation but are not in fact very valuable to it. They include such things as having to attend meetings that are largely a waste of some attendees' time; having to write reports that are unnecessarily detailed or long or that no-one actually reads or acts upon; being copied in on emails that are of minor relevance but require people to read them in order to know that they are of minor relevance, and so on … does this ring any bells? In Towergate we describe these activities as 'Institutionalised Time-Wasters.'

- Quadrant 3 Activities (Proactive-Low Value) These activities are self-chosen but not productive. They include such things as being disorganised (which is essentially a choice) to the point of compromising effectiveness; choosing to focus on 'Could Do's' when 'Must Do's' or 'Should Do's' are clearly present; doing things to 'Gold Standard' when 'Silver Standard ' or 'Bronze Standard' are adequate; doing what we enjoy doing (we call these activities 'Occupational Hobbies') rather than what is most important for the business and so on.

- Quadrant 4 Activities (Proactive-High Value) These activities are (usually) voluntary but they are highly valuable. They include such things as undertaking root cause problem-solving rather than engaging in continuous (often never-ending) fire-fighting, carrying out disaster recover planning before a disaster happens, doing ongoing process analysis and improvement planning, doing systematic service enhancement planning, asking 'what if?' questions and so on. These are activities that the majority of organisations do not build into the majority of peoples' job descriptions and, as most people 'only do what gets them kissed or kicked', they often do not get done at all. The reasons for this are fairly straightforward, people are simply too busy dealing with here-and-now pressures to think of proactively managing the mid and long-term future (which is what Quadrant 4 activities are essentially about). People will certainly get kicked if they are not managing today or tomorrow or next week effectively, but managing the mid and long-term future? Usually the future has to manage itself.

Time Sinks

We know of no systematic study that focuses on the time people actually spend in each of the quadrants above but our own ad-hoc experience suggests the following:

- The average line-manager spends around 70% of their time in Quadrant 1.
- They spend around 15% of their time in Quadrant. 2.
- They spend around 10% of their time in Quadrant 3.
- They spend around 5% of their time in Quadrant 4.

We stress that these figures are experience-driven estimates but we believe they are unlikely to be wildly inaccurate. They also apply only to time spent actually focused on clear 'work' activities (as opposed to social communication, travelling, waiting around etc).

What the figures reveal is that Quadrant 2 and 3 (Low Value) activities may very well account for somewhere in the region of 25% of an individual line manager's working time. That's 25% wasted time!

Clearly there is significant room for improvement here.

Firstly we are in complete control of Quadrant 3, after all these are activities we freely choose to engage in (including being toxically disorganised!)

Possible Quadrant 2 activities (Institutionalised Time Wasters) must be challenged as to their actual worth. If found wanting they must be streamlined or eliminated altogether.

Any time saved through a critical evaluation of Quadrant 2 and 3 activities should be invested in additional Quadrant 4 activities, which should eventually impact positively on the time spent in Quadrant 1 – a truly virtuous circle!

Goals

Most people have goals in life. Even when they don't have clearly expressed ideas of what they do want they usually know what they don't want. Most of us don't want to be ill for example or unhappy or without adequate finances to pay our way. These are 'avoidance goals' so-named for obvious reasons. For many people avoidance goals are the only goals in the armoury. The serious problem with avoidance goals is that they don't help individuals or organisations clarify what they really want to achieve, they just keep them focused on avoiding getting what they don't want.

Someone who has an avoidance goal linked to income for example may remain in an unsatisfying job because they fear the possible financial risks associated with moving to a more satisfying one. A preponderance of avoidance goals tends to hold individuals and organisations back from achieving their full potential.

'Achievement goals' on the other hand are focused on what individuals and organisations really wish to achieve rather than what they want to avoid.

Achievement goals help individuals and organisations focus clearly on what they seek to accomplish. Of course there needs to be a sensible balance between 'avoidance goals' and 'achievement goals'. Deciding to throw up a successful and lucrative business career in order to become a busker on the basis of watching one episode of 'Pop Idol' may not be the most rational course of action to pursue!

High achieving individuals and organisations tend to maintain a practical balance between avoidance and achievement goals, but achievement goals always take priority in terms of focus and drive. Achievement goals give people and organisations a clear sense of direction and purpose, without them we inevitably become reactive and essentially aimless. As an old adage aptly observes,

'Nobody ever gets to the top of mount Everest by wandering around in Nepal!'

When individuals and organisations take the time to really clarify their achievement goals the simple act of doing so probably increase their actual achievement potential by around ten percent.

The 'Knowing-Doing Gap'

Of course if the simple act of clarifying achievement goals guaranteed personal and business success then the world would be populated with hordes of happy and successful individuals. If only!

Something commonly happens in the space between the clarification of personal and organisational goals and their actual achievement. This phenomenon is so well known in academic circles that two eminent professors at the renowned Stanford Graduate School of Business, Jeffrey Pfeffer and Robert Sutton, have given it a name, they've even written a 312 page book about it: *The Knowing-Doing Gap.*

The Knowing-Doing Gap is at the heart of much failure. The majority of individuals and organisations know what they need to do in order to achieve the goals they seek, yet they somehow just don't quite get around to doing them.

Take losing weight as a practical example. Losing weight is a never-ending quest for many people, but everyone knows exactly how it can be achieved – consume fewer calories than your body burns. If you do this you will lose weight, that is absolutely guaranteed for normal people. Therefore if we wish to weigh less than we currently do there are essentially two options open to us: we can either choose to consume fewer calories than we currently do or burn off more calories than we currently do.

It is as simple as that. On paper!

The problem of course is that many things can be made to look pretty simple on paper, for example:

What does a soccer team need to do in order to win matches?
Always score one more goal than the opposition. Simple as that.
How can someone give up smoking?
By not lighting up another cigarette. Ever. Simple
How can people avoid becoming addicted to drugs.
'Just say no.' Simple.
How can managers get the best from their people?
Motivate them and lead by example. Simple as that.

Hundreds, probably thousands, of books, DVDs, magazine articles and CD-roms are published on the topic of managing and running businesses every year. There are also hundreds of management and leadership courses available. They all say essentially the same things and in the main they offer sound and sensible advice. As the average manager may read one business book a year, three or four business articles and also attend seminars or short courses on effective management we need to ask ourselves why there are still so many poor managers around (you could probably think of one or two right now if you put your mind to it.) With such a plethora of sound advice available why aren't more managers and organisations putting it into practice? The answer to this conundrum lies in understanding the roots of the Knowing-Doing Gap.

Short-Term, Long-Term

The roots of the Knowing-Doing gap are set deep within the soil of human nature. People in general prefer short-term returns to long-term ones and quick fixes over root-cause problem solving. We aren't very good at delaying our immediate gratification needs either, a fact that advertisers understand very well.

'Why wait for that new Car / TV / Sofa / Expensive Gadget? Just take out a loan with us (at 30000% APR) and it can be yours RIGHT NOW!'

The problem is that the overwhelming majority of genuinely worthwhile goals require persistence and effort to achieve. Usually its easier to go for a quick fix. As we will describe in a later section it is psychologically more comfortable to do nothing about many problems than it is to confront them. In addition many worthwhile goals require an investment of time, effort and resources that will not show any immediate return. In fact quite the opposite often happens.

Two common examples are given below.

What will a thirty-year-old-thirty-a-day smoker get if he or she decides to give up cigarettes?
Immediate punishment from nicotine withdrawal.
And when will the main benefits kick in?
Months, maybe even years in the future.

What happens if a line manager decides to confront a long-serving but poorly-performing staff member?
Immediate grief.
And when will the main benefits come?
Who knows?

These are practical examples of the real-life difficulties people can face if they choose to pursue a worthwhile goal. It is not surprising therefore that many back off from decisions such as these, it's a lot easier to walk away. The fact remains however that genuinely worthwhile goals almost always necessitate considerable resolve, substantial investment (of time, money or effort) and a resolute belief in the value of the journey. Many people desire worthwhile long-term goals but find it extremely difficult to sustain the effort required to achieve them. They are not unusual. The certain promise of Jam today can be much more compelling than the uncertain promise of Caviar in twelve months time!

There have been numerous occasions during the Economic-Towergate journey when 'Jam today' was a real option for the senior management team. However Peter Cullum's commitment to the long-term has ensured that the quest for organisational Caviar continues!

CHAPTER 3

Reflections

*Make everything as simple as possible,
but not simpler.*

Albert Einstein

As Towergate has developed and grown (much faster than anyone originally envisaged) we have consistently attempted to identify any 'enduring management truths' that may have become apparent as a result of our various experiences, decisions and actions. We have clearly been successful (to date!) in our ventures, yet the extraordinary rate of change involved, propelled, as ever, by the exceptional drive of Peter Cullum, has meant that most stages of the journey have been highly unstructured, often revolutionary and, seemingly, driven primarily by sheer *momentum*.

'*Reflect too much and you're dead*' became something of a mantra as the frenetic pace of development accelerated, and it appears, by and large, to have been an effective dictum.

Yet despite the raw pragmatism of this approach our desire to illuminate any hidden structure and to identify any underlying management principles continued to gnaw. We were after all classically trained managers, taught to deal with complex business problems in structured and logical ways. Yet here we were rushing from purchase to purchase, negotiation to negotiation, decision to decision, thinking on our feet without pausing for breath and often feeling like deranged contestants in some bizarre business Game Show.

But were we really managing by animal instinct alone or had all those years of formal training and development become sufficiently embedded in our subconscious minds to make the control of the complex instinctive and second nature?

What our conscious minds perceived often appeared chaotic, anarchic and frantic: in a word 'unmanageable.' But what of our subconscious minds? Did we simply take it all in and then calmly select appropriate mantras seized from long forgotten brain-files marked 'management', albeit at breakneck speed? Could we genuinely ascribe the application of established management principles and theories to the turmoil of this seemingly chaotic 'real world' experience?

We instinctively understood that it would be extremely useful to have a clear and systematic analysis of the ways in which we worked through the complex challenges and trials involved in the development of Towergate in order that any generic management principles or maxims could be distilled and disseminated. In particular we wished to understand how Cullum made sense of it all and managed to lead the business forward as rapidly and effectively as he did. Which if any underlying management principles or decision algorithms did he apply? The essential question was this: could we distil the essence of the 'Cullum Management Method' and pass it on to the next generation of Towergate leaders?

Professional Broking April 2005

The consolidator consolidates

ProfessionalBroking

The management magazine for insurance brokers   April 2005

Consolidation focus
From preparing to sell, to market forecasts

Round Table
Rates, regulation and cost transparency top the agenda

ProfessionalBroking
SENTIMENT SURVEYS
Latest results of the brokers' barometer

Pushing the boundaries
Peter Cullum on Towergate's expansion plans despite concerns about it growing too fast

These are deep questions of course and we do not pretend to have any easy or glib answers to them. Rather, in analysing our experiences in depth, we have become increasingly drawn to a clearer understanding of the processes, both physical and psychological, which underly all human decisions and actions. On reflection we can see that these processes played key roles (often unconsciously) in influencing the ways in which we responded to the complexities involved in managing the growth of Towergate. We have come to believe that these underlying physical and psychological processes are endemic to all key management challenges and what follows is our brief attempt to describe and understand the most pertinent of them.

Systems Theory

In the introduction to this book we described four common genres of management writing. One of them, *'Business Management is Very Very Complex'* is worth considering in more detail.

Complexity is undoubtedly increasing and complex entities such as organisations, economic systems, human beings and the processes of management and leadership themselves can all be viewed and understood through an almost infinite variety of possible 'lenses'. One such lens is *Systems Theory*.

A definition of Systems Theory is given below:

Systems Theory: the transdisciplinary study of the abstract organization of phenomena, independent of their substance, type, or spatial or temporal scale of existence. It investigates both the principles common to all complex entities, and the (usually mathematical) models which can be used to describe them.

Source: Principia Cybernetica

Sounds a hoot doesn't it! What it implies in plain English is that we can understand complex systems by analysing their underlying processes and applying appropriate mathematical models. To a certain extent this is true, but only to the extent that a complex system actually does behave in logically or mathematically consistent ways.

A computer programme for example is logically and mathematically consistent and can be fully described and understood in terms of its underlying decision algorithms. The same principle applies to a motor car, a television set or even a space shuttle. We can understand how they work in terms of appropriate mathematical and physical laws. The power and undeniable successes of Systems Theory (the 'Dismal Science' of Economics not withstanding!) in helping us understand complexity has almost inevitably led to its application in the fields of business and management.

During the 1980's and early 1990's Total Quality Management (TQM) became *the* business bandwagon to be on. TQM, in management terms, is Systems Theory writ large and during this period Gurus such as W Edwards Deming and Joseph Juran (previously ignored by Western businesses but revered in Japan) were suddenly lauded as demigods and their particular varieties of TQM championed with quasi-religious zeal. Nowadays of course things are different. TQM is 'sooooo' yesterday as far as business fads are concerned and, as every aspiring CEO quickly recognises, career suicide awaits those foolish enough to utter a dead buzzword in earshot of senior management!

This (unfortunately common) 'three-years-and-it's-past-its-sell-by-date' approach to management and organizational theory can be extremely counterproductive (as we will see later).

TQM was however a vital ingredient in saving Economic insurance in the early 1990's. It expressed a viewpoint of the business that every member of staff could appreciate and recognise and it helped develop the notion of the 'Federal Structure' that was taken forward into Towergate. In a business that had for years fundamentally missed its reason for existence TQM techniques got back down to basics.

The application of simple yet effective job-analysis and process-mapping tools provided ample evidence of the failings of the Economic machine at all levels.

It was not uncommon for example to find two people doing very similar jobs in totally different ways. On one occasion we discovered that a particular underwriting department employed an individual to produce (manually) a set of returns which were passed to a claims department that promptly filed them in the bin! The claims department concerned had no use for these figures, in fact they had not used for them for a number of years, but it was assumed that the stats were automatically generated by a mechanical run and that it was more trouble than it was worth to stop receiving them. The straightforward TQM techniques of process analysis and process mapping identified and put an end to this and many other anomalies within the business.

There will of course be similar examples of ineffective working practices occurring inside Towergate right now (not too many we hope!) or indeed inside any sizeable business that you care to analyse using basic TQM principles. One clear and practical example springs to mind.

A particularly large and valuable Towergate business unit once faced a very serious operational crisis. However, the first that 'head office' knew about the problem was the threatened mass-resignation (on a Friday evening!) of

EVERY single employee – and all this despite the ritual of monthly management reporting!

The core problem, it transpired, was rather prosaic. For some reason the office telephones had begun ringing continuously, preventing routine administration taking place. File backlogs and resulting stress levels were rising exponentially and both staff and customers were feeling the heat. Something needed to be done to rectify the situation, and BDQ. But what exactly?

'We know,' said the staff, 'we need more people to answer the phones.' QED!

'Hang about,' said management, 'it's only been a gentle increase in policy count from last year, you must be doing something different, or doing something wrong.' QED!

Highly emotional impasse. Threatened mass resignation. Emergency dialogue with senior management. During the ensuing discussions one simple question hit pay dirt. It emerged that incoming telephone calls had trebled in volume in just two months and this was the root-cause of the workflow problems.

The pay-dirt question was this: *what are these increased telephone calls about?*

'*We know what they're about*' said staff, '*people want to know how to pay their premiums!*'

'*They want to know how to pay their premiums!!!???* *But we make that easy for them … don't we?*'

Our standard renewal notice would, obviously, have included straightforward details on how to pay the premium? Yes? No-brainer? Yes?

Think again!

A cursory inspection of the office printer, and the myriad renewal notices emanating thereof, instantly disabused us of that assumption. Not one of the renewals included a Remittance Advice Sheet, the "how to pay" bit!

Nor had they for at least the previous two months following some 'routine' programming changes that had majestically contrived to eliminate the payment page completely.

So, hadn't anyone checked that all was OK following the programming changes?

Yes, actually, they had.

Management had carried out *technical* audits of the printer output *on screen* following the programming changes but no-one with any experience had looked at what was *actually* coming out of the printer and being sent to our customers. That little job was delegated to a temporary school leaver who, to be frank, would not have noticed if the print-outs had been in Mandarin Chinese, or Klingon for that matter. Everyone had simply (and understandably) *assumed* that what was on the print-out screen was also on the printer hard copy.

Such assumptions can be dangerous! How many similar assumptions may exist in your own organisation?

We didn't call it a formal TQM review but that's what we carried out across the Group after that particular episode! One month later we had a pile of paper-based communications that were regularly sent to our customers, probably at least a foot in depth, which could only be described as utter garbage. Lots of lessons were learned!

Along the way we also unearthed a disturbing piece of information that we are continually attempting to overcome – many staff have little or no idea of the true functionality of the software they use.

Again a practical example may illustrate; staff in one particular Towergate business presented their IT department with a wish list of improvements that would make their lives easier. The vast majority of their requests focused on specific functions that the existing software (ostensibly) could not do.

Readers may (or perhaps may not) be surprised to learn that subsequent to the IT Manager being confronted with these shortcomings and verbally mugged for allowing the business to be crippled by ineffective software, he was able to demonstrate that in 90% of the requests raised the software actually could do the job required (and he proved it there and then) and that in the remaining 10% a simple adjustment was all that was necessary.

The reality was that we, management, only gave our non-IT people the essential skills (as we saw them) to carry out 'priority' tasks in the shortest possible time. However, as the range of these tasks (inevitably) expanded and the process intelligence requirements increased, we often left staff adrift without effective support. The result was a small army of gifted twenty-somethings all coming up with their own personal 'work-arounds' for overcoming specific problems- a clear recipe for chaos!

This was our fault, not theirs and it taught us that TQM, or any systems-based approach to management, can only add value when basic people-support mechanisms are in place.

Key Lessons: continuously question your assumptions. Map the key processes in your business, especially those that impact directly on your customers. Regularly review the communications you actually send to your customers. Provide excellent IT and systems training for your staff.

Bad Thinking

The whole phenomenon of 'Management Fads' and so-called 'Management Speak' (often derived from systems theory) has left a sour taste in many people's mouths, particularly those whose livelihoods have been badly affected by passing fads such 'downsizing' 're-engineering' or 'optimising'. Many managers (and practically all non-managerial staff) are extremely sceptical of such things.

Our view is that the overwhelming majority of fads fail for one of two principal reasons. Either they are completely loopy from the outset (the use of Calligraphy and Feng-Shui as management tools spring to mind) or they fail to recognise the inherent 'messiness' of most business and management activities.

All logically consistent theories will work ... in theory! The problem of course is that the real world is rarely (if ever) the neat-and-tidy-everything-fits place that theory requires it to be. The real world of business and management is awash with illogicalities, improbabilities, chance events and, by far the most volatile factor of all, people. People can be irrational – and yes, that is a deliberate understatement!

In a world comprised of entirely rational individuals we would have no real need for managers or leaders – and that is precisely why we do!

Irrational thinking and illogical decision-making can sometimes border on the surreal.

Recall the Hoover 'free-flights' fiasco? Various free air-fares (some worth up to £500) were promised on the purchase of a £99 Hoover vacuum cleaner (the cheapest option to trigger the reward). The offer was made on the (erroneous) assumptions that the public would fail to read through the voluminous small print that limited their actual choices and that the travel agencies involved in the promotion would be able to sell expensive add-ons which would offset the flight costs. Wrong.

It just didn't happen that way and when David Dixon, a disgruntled horse-trainer from High Seaton in Cumbria, kidnapped a Hoover van in protest at not receiving the flights he had been promised, he became a national hero overnight.

The resulting debacle cost Hoover millions in financial damages and in all probability earned them a brand-curse that will last for decades.

And while we're on the topic of illogical decisions, what about the following:

- Giving Trader Nick Leeson back and front office authority at Barings Singapore – which led to the Bank's collapse?
- The UK Government's Poll-Tax – one of the most un-popular taxes of modern times?
- Sir Clive Sinclair's three-wheeled electric car?
- Believing that the new Wembley stadium would be ready for the 2006 FA cup final?
- Or that it would be on budget?

We could continue!

But then again, what about Akio Morita's 'irrational' belief that the Sony Walkman would be a roaring success? Or James Dyson's revolutionary redesign of the humble vacuum cleaner?

Our inherent tendency to buck the trend is both a curse and a blessing. Sometimes, when we go with a gut feeling and against the odds, we screw up, yet at other times we can hit the jackpot. Most 'systems' approaches severely under-estimate the extent and depth of human irrationality, in both its positive and negative expressions, as we shall see later.

Many management theories (and managers for that matter) succumb to the comforting notion that business are similar to cause and effect 'machines' or mechanical systems. Instigate steps one to thirty-three of the current guru's sales and marketing plan/change management plan/project management plan – in other words pull all the right levers - and success will follow as night follows day. Unfortunately businesses are not simply mechanical systems.

In some ways the challenges we face in managing businesses are similar to those confronting theoretical physics where mechanistic Newtonian principles and chaotic quantum effects, the bedrocks of our understanding of the physical world, often contradict each other totally. Newtonian Mechanics is excellent at predicting the behaviours of large objects such as planets, aeroplanes, satellites or motor cars. When it comes to the sub-atomic level however Newtonian Mechanics breaks down completely and we are then faced with fundamental unpredictability, randomness and seriously bizarre but allowable events (such as an electron being in two different places at exactly the same time or simultaneously being both an intangible wave and a concrete particle.)

The management environment is akin to a combination of the Newtonian and Quantum worlds, on some occasions the lever-pulling, mechanistic, cause-and-effect model works admirably, but on others it does not.

This is not to imply that 'academic' or 'mechanistic' approaches to understanding business and management are of little value, but it must be said that management theories often underestimate the unpredictabilities of the real world, including the role that chance events play in success and failure. Recall our earlier mythical ice-cream vendors for example or consider the fate of all those carefully designed new products, services and marketing drives that were meticulously developed and primed for high-impact launch on September 12th 2001. Time and chance again.

Academic business theory, planning and thorough analysis are of course necessary. They are necessary but frequently insufficient to guarantee business success. Room has to be made for chance events, for the 'law of unexpected consequences' (consider Iraq) and for human irrationality. The real world is not the logically consistent algorithm of the business school case study and it would be truly interesting to see how well many prominent academic theorists would actually perform as real managers operating in real 'in-your-face' business contexts. A large part of Peter Cullum's success undoubtedly stems from his ability to tolerate (to thrive on) gargantuan levels of ambiguity and uncertainty and to 'go with gut feelings' in situations that would render the vast majority of mortals psychologically immobile.

Many organisations are risk-adverse and tend to fall into accepted ways of doing things. People such as Cullum, who tend to occasionally 'buck the system', are traditionally punished when their innovations do not work out and ignored when they do. In this way serious innovation and creative thinking are expunged from the organisation's repertoire.

Such considerations aside, it would be remiss of us to suggest that academic theories have little or nothing to offer the real-world manager. Even taking due note of the time-worn adage that *'those who can, do, while those who can't, teach'* it is clear that management theorists have contributed a great deal to our understanding of the ways in which businesses function.

Key Lessons: Beware of management 'Fads' and 'flavour of the month' theories, many have kernels of truth in them but they often go too far. Take from them what works but always remember that business is 'messy' and chance events will also impact on your results. Be prepared to adapt the 'master plan' if it isn't working or if unexpected events render it defunct (the creation of Folgate – the insurance broking business created by Cullum to harness distribution – in 2001 for example was seriously affected by the tragic events of September 11th which shifted risk-tolerance dramatically.)

Make sure that any important decisions (especially group-made decisions) are rigorously questioned and challenged before being implemented. Beware of 'group-think' and don't gloss over any potential down-sides. Give your most important plans a thorough grilling before implementing them.

Launch of Folgate at the Natural History Museum 2002
Left to right: Tony Proverbs, Peter Cullum, Andy Homer, Kenny Maciver

Winners and Losers

Are you a winner or a loser? More crucially, are you *perceived* as being a winner or a loser? This is an important distinction as you no doubt appreciate. The key question of course is this - what makes some people winners and others losers?

Ability? Well, that depends. Recall the (hypothetical) case of our two intrepid ice-cream sellers detailed earlier in this book. One succeeded through good fortune, the other went bust due to its opposite. But which individual had the greater true ability? If both had started their businesses in the same (good) year, who would ultimately have sold the most ice-cream? And whose business would have lasted longest?

We have no way of knowing. Bad luck scuppered our 2004 starter before any real progress could be made. Ten years down the line however each may be remembered very differently - one as a 'winner' the other as a 'loser'. In many situations such vagaries of chance (there it is again) impact on everyone equally, so there is something of a level playing field in place. But what about other situations?

Let's consider a few.

Was it You, or was it the Horse?

What proportion of a horse-racing jockey's success will ultimately be down to the quality of the horses he gets to ride?

Imagine imposing a rule on the most successful jockeys (let's say the top twenty performers in any given year) that made it mandatory for them to ride the horse that had the lowest 'form' in fifty percent of all the races they enter during the following twelve months. That would probably shake things up a bit in the Jockey league-tables. It's pretty difficult to win a thoroughbred race on a (relative) mule! However, if a jockey still managed to finish fairly high in the winner ratings even when in a 'fifty percent mules' year, then you would probably be looking at undeniable racing talent.

In some instances a person's level of 'success' will be heavily influenced by factors external to the person themselves. Horse racing is clearly one instance, so too is motor racing. A Formula One driver won't win the World Championship in a car that can only make it to the end of sixty percent of Grand Prix events.

But what about other competitive activities, such as tennis or football? How much of a top player's success in these sports can be attributed to non-personal factors. Very little probably. You won't get to play tennis like Roger Federer or football like Wayne Rooney by stealing their racquets or boots! Federer and Rooney are almost totally 'independent' of the equipment they use (you could part-scupper them by de-tensioning the racquets and de-studding the boots of course, but even then they'd probably perform in the top ten percent!)

Organisations, and the people who lead and manage them, sometimes fail to appreciate the role that non-personal factors can play in generating people's successes and failures. For example does the current 'Salesperson of the Year' genuinely deserve the accolades he or she has received, or was the fact that they were riding one of the best horses in the race (in terms of territory, number of prospects, quality of prospects, back-up marketing support, sales management support, coaching etc) a rather important factor too? And similarly with the lowest performer, can we be really sure that he or she is in reality a 'dud' - or could it partly be down to the 'horse' they've been obliged to get onto? Difficult to tell sometimes, easier to tell other times, but it is a consideration that all managers should keep in mind when analysing performance and assessing potential.

We accept that there is a downside in taking this approach to understanding differences in performance. The easiest cop-out for any individual charged with poor workmanship is to go straight for the tools (or the horse) :

> *'It was the IT system that caused me to miss budget boss, it's crap!'*

We've all heard (and probably used) similar excuses ourselves, but these and other possible limitations withstanding, Systems Theory, and TQM in particular, have given managers an increased awareness of the ways in which processes and process variations affect outcomes. Some of these are detailed in our next section.

Understanding Processes

Everything that exists has been produced by a process. The galaxy, the solar system, the Earth, all living things, Towergate and, of course, this book. In order to truly understand outcomes, be they sales results, football results or election results, we need to understand the processes that generate them. This is a considerable challenge but, thankfully, we do not need to get into the rocket science to appreciate some important concepts; one of the most useful of these concepts is process *variation*.

Special and Random causes of Variation in Process Outcomes

No process can ever be perfect. That is to say no two *outcomes* of any process will ever be *exactly* the same. No matter how refined, quality controlled, or hi-tech a process is, there will inevitably be variations in what it produces. Take two samples of the most expensive watch in the world and you will find that they won't keep time at *exactly* the same rate. It may take two or three hundred years (or maybe even two or three thousand) to notice any discernable difference, but there will be a difference. Each watch will have been produced by exactly the same quality-controlled-to-death process, but tiny anomalies will creep in. Miniscule variations in the physical make up of the component parts, in they ways they are manufactured or in the ways they are assembled and work together will inevitably translate into differences at the operational level. The same applies to motor cars. No two examples of the same model will ever deliver *exactly* the same fuel consumption or *exactly* the same acceleration figures. Again the differences will probably be very small, but they will be there none the less. And if there are differences in the outcomes of these extremely well-controlled processes, imagine the variation that results when process control is not good or even missing altogether!

Some examples: even though the plans they are given may be identical, no two builders will build *exactly* the same garage, or patio or conservatory. Similarly with hairdressers, teachers and managers. Given precisely the same sets of objectives, different individuals will inevitably generate different outcomes.

Variation in process outcomes is therefore inevitable, but it is crucial to appreciate the central differences between the causes of such variations. Some practical examples will hopefully illustrate the point.

Imagine that a truly world-class runner, tennis player or swimmer finishes fourth or fifth in a competition that he or she should really have 'walked'. What could have caused this unexpected outcome to occur? Essentially there are two possibilities, the first (and most common) is that something *specific* caused the unexpected result. Maybe the individual concerned had some sort of physical or psychological impairment on the day – a slight virus infection perhaps, or a niggling worry that affected their focus or commitment to win.

In theory such *special causes of variation* could be identified after an unexpected failure and measures could then be put in place in order to prevent them affecting performance in the future. Special causes of variation in process outcomes can be identified and in theory eliminated.

But what if there were no clearly apparent (special) causes for the poor performance? What if the individual concerned had been one hundred percent fit and one hundred percent committed to winning? How can we explain the poor result in this case?

In order to attempt such an explanation we must take into account the *total* process factors involved in either winning or losing and not just those that apply to the individual concerned.

The total process factors will include all the other competitors, the weather, the track or court or pool, the equipment used and so on.

Imagine for example that a number of other competitors just happened to be particularly focused on the day concerned and had trained much harder than they normally trained. Imagine also that our world class athlete/tennis player/swimmer was in fact only 99.999 percent match fit and only 99.999 percent match focused, differences that would be too slight to register, but there all the same. Imagine also that the physical conditions for our world-class player (the lane they were running or swimming in or the particular ends of the court they happened to be playing in) were slightly less favourable to them on the day than the physical conditions the other competitors experienced (maybe there were slight wind or temperature differences etc.) Imagine also that our world class contender's shoes or racquet or swimming gear was slightly less effective that day than normal while those of the other contenders happened to be spot on. This is a lot of 'ifs' we accept, but such things happen more often than we realise. Each miniscule difference has only a slight effect but when many of them come together they can have a significant influence on outcomes.

These chance events are called *random* causes of variation and there is absolutely nothing we can do about them. Every process is susceptible to them and every once in a while they will inevitably 'gang up' to produce extraordinary outcomes – for good or bad.

Hopefully therefore it is clear that the causes of

particular process outcomes may not always be as straightforward as we are inclined to think. We need to understand the differences between 'special' and 'random' causes of variation otherwise we may see special causes where in fact mainly random ones are present, and vice-versa. This has serious implications. Many (most?) managers associate performance (good and bad) almost exclusively with the performer.

'She's this quarter's best-performing salesperson because she's excellent at closing deals' (a special cause of variation) or

'He's our worst-performing salesperson this quarter because he doesn't push hard enough for the sale.' (another special cause).

These observations may be true or they may be only partly-true explanations for the outcomes concerned. In order to be really sure about what caused the sales results (good and bad) we would need to know whether the star performer had benefited from a bunch of helpful random causes this quarter while the poor performer was on the receiving end of a clutch of demonic ones? This is potentially hard work we accept. It is often difficult enough to assess the genuine causes of performance differences when we do not take total process variations into account, but being aware of the possible effects that special external factors may have on results may help us make better decisions overall. Food for thought for all managers!

Cullum consistently analyses the factors underlying performance variation (both good and bad). Most of the time his judgment on the root causes of such variation is spot on. On numerous occasions he has seen opportunities when everyone else in the room has seen only problems. He has an uncanny knack of knowing whether an under-performing business is fixable, i.e. that the under-performance stems from special (fixable) causes rather than endemic (non-fixable) ones.

Key Lessons: always appreciate that results are influenced by many factors. 'Success' and 'failure' are not always down to people's efforts or talents alone. Ensure that everyone has a 'level playing field'. True talent will succeed even when underlying conditions are not favourable. Don't always accept the 'bad tools' explanation for poor performance but also appreciate that many people see performance problems as being caused by factors external to themselves.

The 'Three P's' Model of Business Performance

In Towergate we use a '3P' model to help us better understand our key business processes and outcomes. It's a pretty straightforward approach but it works for us. The details are given below:

BUSINESS OUTCOMES = PRODUCTS x PROCESSES x PEOPLE

Note that there is a multiplier between each 'P' in the above equation. If any variable approaches zero the whole business outcome approaches zero also (99 x 99 x 0 = 0).

Excellent products combined with horrendous processes or inept people won't get you far. And no matter how good your people are they won't succeed if they have to sell uncompetitive products through limited distribution channels.

At Towergate we consider the most important variable in the equation, and by a very wide margin indeed, to be people. Excellent products and processes can always be replicated by competitors (note the success of the Chinese in this arena) but excellent people cannot. Excellent people will endeavour to overcome the vagaries of less-than-perfect processes, be they poor IT systems, bad claims handling procedures or even something as banal as limited photocopying resources. Excellent people will usually find or make work-arounds where there are process or material deficiencies, at least in the short or medium term. History is replete with examples of armies and individuals who have made the most of inferior weapons and equipment and vanquished a technically or numerically superior foe.

The implications of the '3P' model can be revealing. For example, if the products we offer are ninety percent ideal in terms of customer requirements and if our people are eighty percent ideal in terms of their skills, knowledge and levels of commitment and if our processes are seventy percent ideal in terms of their efficiency and effectiveness, then we are still producing only just above fifty percent of a theoretically achievable perfect outcome ($0.9 \times 0.8 \times 0.7 = 0.504$ or just 50.4%!)

The theoretically achievable outcome of one hundred percent effectiveness and efficiency will never be attained in the real world of course because people, processes and products can never be absolutely perfect. But it is instructive (and sometimes terrifying) to have a stab at estimating where the organisation's current performance level is in relation to this theoretical ideal. One of the endemic problems Towergate has to contend with is IT variation. 127 acquisitions to date means managing in excess of 50 legacy systems – quite a challenge in our ongoing attempt to continuously ratchet up our operational effectiveness!

In many real-world instances Products, Processes and People fall well below the effectiveness/efficiency ratios quoted above. For example at a seventy percent level of effectiveness/efficiency across the board the resulting outcome for the three P's overall (0.7 x 0.7 x 0.7) falls to less than thirty-five percent of its theoretically achievable ideal.

Our current estimate of the overall effectiveness of Towergate as measured by the 3P equation is somewhere in the region of 38% to 42%. In all probability we are doing relatively well in relation to industry averages, but there is clearly opportunity for significant improvement.

Underperformance: Playing The Blame Game

The 3P model can also help us understand crucial differences in people's perceptions of the root causes of underperformance in organisations. Underperformance is commonly viewed very differently by people working at different levels within organisational hierarchies.

At the point where a perceived underperformance actually occurs, be it within sales, customer service, claims handling, marketing, underwriting etc, the root cause of the problem is commonly (almost always, in truth) seen as being a resource issue. In other words, and in terms of the 3P model, underperformance is seen as being a Product and/or Processes issue rather than a People one. A common lament at this level is:

> '...*underperformance is not our fault, it's because we're understaffed / underesourced / underbudgeted / underinformed / undersupported ...*'

As we move up the organisational hierarchy however the root cause of underperformance is increasingly seen as being predominantly a People problem rather than a Product or Process one. The common 'management' response to the lament above is:

> '*...we're not so sure about that frankly , we think you could use your existing resources more effectively.*'

This massive (and it commonly is massive) difference between perceptions of the root causes of underperformance lies at the heart of much misunderstanding and bad feeling between people working at different levels within organisational hierarchies.

Ask the CEO or senior management team of any business whether or not they believe that the resources provided to their staff are 'adequate for purpose' and you will most likely get a variation of the following in response,

> '*...we know there is some room for improvement in certain areas but overall we compare very well with industry norms ...*'

...or something to that effect.

Ask the same question of a front-line employee however and you will be likely to receive a very different response indeed!

So who is right?

Unfortunately this is largely an unanswerable question as it involves individual perceptions and underlying psychological processes. We will consider a few of these in the sections that follow.

Key Lessons: business outcomes are influenced by three key factors; people, products and processes, a weakness in any one can impact dramatically on

end results. People are the most important factor influencing success. There is commonly a massive difference in perception regarding the root causes of under-performance. At the operational level people commonly see underperformance as being a resource issue ('we don't have adequate people / telephones / computers / printers / floor space etc.) As we move up the organisational hierarchy however the causes of underperformance tend to be seen as a utilisation issue ('you can get more out of what you've got'). Understand these differences in perception, each usually has some substance, and work together to reach a compromise.

Us and Them

It will be useful to complete the following exercise (taken from one of Towergate's Management Development Programmes) before reading further.

1. Think for a moment about someone with whom you do not have a good working relationship (hopefully 650 potential candidates do not readily spring to mind at this point!)

   Now think about a time when this individual displayed 'difficult' behaviour(s) at work.

   What, in your view, were the underlying reason(s) for this individual displaying the difficult behaviour(s) concerned?

   Briefly jot down your views.

2. Now, accepting that no-one (not even our good selves) is perfect, think about an occasion when you behaved (at

work) in a way that was not very constructive.

Briefly jot down the reason(s) why you behaved this way.

If you are a normal human being rather than a saint or a psychopath then in all probability you will have assigned quite different causes to the non-constructive behaviours emitting from yourself and others.

The vast majority of people commonly attribute their own non-constructive behaviours to *impersonal* and *temporary* causes.

> *'I behaved badly on that occasion because I was under extreme pressure from my boss / I hadn't slept properly for two nights / I was jet-lagged / I had a migraine coming on ... etc.'*

This is a very common response when analysing our own shortcomings. When people extrapolate the reasons for the shortcomings of others however they often attribute them to *personal* and *permanent* causes.

> *'He/she behaved badly on that occasion because he/she is... a bully / a control freak / devious / irrational ... etc.'*

In other words when I behave badly it's because *I've* had a shitty day, but when *they* behave badly it's because *they're* shits!

Perceptual inconsistencies such as these lie at the heart of much of the 'them and us' challenges which affect all organisations to some degree. The bad news is that they are rooted in core psychological processes and are probably impossible to eradicate completely. It's just the way human beings are, 'in groups' and 'out groups' ('Us' and 'Them') will inevitably view each other through different lenses. No matter how moral, open or equitable we attempt make our organisations a percentage of staff will still suspect dark machinations in the boardroom.

Now look back at your own responses to scenarios 1 and 2 above and reflect on whether you too are quite normal in the ways in which you attribute causes to the non-constructive behaviours of yourself and others!

An awareness of basic perceptual differences such as those described above, and others we do not have time or space to detail here, should at least help us understand and deal more effectively with common organisational impasses, even if we cannot remove them completely

To return to the 'it's a resource problem / it's a people problem' perspectives on the root causes of underperformance described previously, it has to be accepted that the 'we need more resources' claim often has an element of credibility to it.

That said however it is a pretty safe bet that you will not encounter too many managers willing to declare that they have precisely the number of staff, quality of IT, level of senior management support and budget allocation necessary to achieve all their objectives!

These and other structural, psychological and communication challenges mean that winning, and more importantly keeping, the 'hearts and minds' of staff will always present considerable challenges. How best we tackle these challenges will be the central topic of the following sections. We are acutely aware in Towergate that despite our success we do not always disseminate our collective experience across the Group. Directors seldom if ever get the opportunity to systematically coach and develop the next generation of leaders, and this is a challenge we will be prioritising in the near future.

> **Key Lessons: human beings tend to perceive themselves and others through different psychological mechanisms. Understanding these differences can help us deal with organisational misperceptions more effectively. However, no matter how hard an organisation tries to 'get everyone on board' in terms of its espoused culture and values it is probably inevitable that some people will remain stubbornly cynical.**

Leadership

How can anyone possibly hope to say anything fresh or newly insightful about leadership? Management theorists have spent entire careers researching the subject. And as for books! Typing the word 'Leadership' into the Amazon business books (UK) search engine resulted (May 2007) in 22,128 titles being displayed. The same search on the US site resulted in 203,840 titles!

Leadership is a perennial hot topic in management theory and the hottest question of all is 'are effective leaders born or 'made'? The 'Nature – Nurture' argument so beloved of psychological researchers.

If the consensus of opinion was that effective leaders are born (its mainly your genes) rather than made (its mainly your experiences) then there would be precious few Leadership books on the market (just as there aren't too many on the subject of 'How To Be Seven Feet Tall' or 'How To Have Three Eyes'.)

Given the plethora of books that do exist, it is clear that their authors believe there is much that individuals can do to enhance their leadership qualities.

This of course is true. It is true of every human attribute that is not rigidly fixed by genetics. We can all become better musicians, golfers, painters, calligraphers, managers and, yes, leaders too, by learning proven techniques and by practising them until they become part of what we are. But this will only take us so far. What separates a Mozart, Shakespeare, Ali, Pele, DaVinci, Michelangelo, Newton or Einstein from mere mortals is their natural and abundant talent. And we do not have to restrict our examples to such obvious geniuses, the same 'rule of talent' applies to all professional musicians, published authors and professional footballers, many may aspire to these positions but few actually achieve them.

Talent is as relevant to leadership as it is to the arts or sport. Some people (not that many unfortunately) are simply naturals. Others 'acquire leadership techniques' and have varying degrees of operational success depending on their predispositions and core personality traits.

We strongly believe that one of the crucial roles executive management has to undertake is to identify exceptional leadership potential within their organisations.

A key concept underpinning the foundation of the Towergate Academy is the identification and nurturing of exceptional leadership talent. Competent leadership matters in all businesses, but exceptional leadership *really* matters.

Leadership, a personal perspective
Andy Homer
CEO, Towergate Partnership

It is hard to imagine many boardrooms containing such items as a Fart Machine and cans of Bullshit Spray, but that's the Towergate way in a nutshell. Irreverent about status and the status quo, anti-political (perpetrators get the BS spray treatment) yet deadly serious about its mission.

Peter Cullum's journey is set out here for all those interested in the realities of business innovation, and for admirers and detractors alike, to check out. Since our paths crossed over 30 years ago, what has consistently distinguished Peter's approach from all other leaders I have worked with is his relentless drive for innovation and improvement. There are no settled diaries, long winded meetings or endless committees here. It's always "up and at 'em" with the prospect of another exciting deal, another opportunity or another new way of doing things ever present.

Those who stand still in Towergate get painted or demolished.

The Towergate culture is bound together by classic adhesive; war stories of deals done and not done; fervent, almost insane presentations to staff and prospective vendors (the Cullum/Homer double-act on the acquisition of Folgate springs to mind!); a strong loyalty to Towergate "believers" that is quasi-religious in connotation, an abiding disrespect for the "it can't be done" syndrome and a focus that puts Customer first, second and third.

Loyalty to business partners and staff, especially staff, comes directly from Peter. We disagree on little of substance, the minor disagreements we occasionally do have usually arise when I tell him that he is being too soft on some people – something many folk might find rather hard to believe!

What makes Towergate work, and what will sustain it for a long time to come, is the people who have been attracted to work for Peter and Paul and Tony and Kenny and me – I hope you get the picture? We tend to recruit people we know and can trust to die in a ditch for us and Towergate. There is an evangelical (back to religion again) spirit around the management group and we have lost no-one – and I mean no-one – we did not want to lose from the group over the past 5 years. Peter gathers about him gatherers of talent, it's pyramid recruiting rather than pyramid selling.

Our Top Team is Champions League talent, with an ever developing strategy second to none in UK insurance and we have truly exceptional people in all of our businesses. Over the next five years there are no boundaries to our ambitions or our ability to become a dominant force in the broader financial services market. Even if it can't be done we'll probably have a go anyway.

Towergate, I remind myself every morning, is so much more fun than work, and that is the best way I can describe this incredible journey with "PGC".

Exceptional Leadership

It is difficult in a publication of this nature, one that tracks the development of a real business and real people, to discuss personalities in terms that do not come across as being sycophantic, exaggerated or self-congratulatory. However if there are lessons to be learned from experiences such as the Towergate journey, and there likely are, then some of the most pertinent ones are concerned with individual personalities and the qualities of exceptional leadership.

It is not unusual for those who possess unusual abilities to have little if any awareness of their origins or forms of expression. Such individuals simply 'do what

Business XL November 2005

"King of Finance King of Fun"

"Peter Cullum is shaking up the insurance sector by injecting a sense of fun, having boldly rejected the rituals of corporate life for the thrill of building his own business. Towergate Partnership is now heading for £2 billion turnover and Cullum has been showered with awards for his achievement."

comes naturally' and it falls to others to attempt to tease out information that may be useful to the rest of us. What follows therefore is Thomas's attempt at analysing the underpinnings of exceptional leadership within the Towergate Partnership.

First of all it must be stated (once again) that Towergate would not exist without Peter Cullum. Everyone involved in the business recognises this fact and no-one has any problem with it. This in itself is an illuminating state of affairs and it speaks volumes about the essential qualities of exceptional leadership. In the sections that follow we will attempt to clarify what these essential qualities are.

Having worked with managers at all levels and in a wide range of organisations and localities Thomas can honestly say that he has rarely if ever witnessed the degree of respect accorded to Peter Cullum, sometimes from individuals who have never even met the man! On the other hand of course there are doubtless others (almost inevitable where exceptional leaders are concerned) who take out their lovingly fashioned 'Cullum-voodoo-dolls' at the end of particularly demanding periods and 'vent!'

One sure indicator of the exceptional leader is that he or she is not universally loved, fierce tribal loyalties just don't work that way, but exceptional leaders are almost always *respected*. Such leaders, as we will see, commonly generate quite extreme emotional responses.

Such practical caveats accepted, if the organisational rumour-machine is, and it probably is, the central vehicle through which a leader's reputation is either made or broken then Peter Cullum has clearly located the Philosopher's Stone, rumour-wise. His past feats, future ambitions, intellectual capabilities, physical energies and all-round-super-hero qualities appear to be growing exponentially as the months and years go by. Thomas has frequently heard the same 'Cullum stories' retold with an inflationary vigour that would make many Banana-Republic economies appear rock-stable. If the process continues much longer mere mortals will have no option other than to communicate with him through a priest.

That said, there really is substance to the rhetoric. The legendary 'Cullum Effect' can be positively alarming in its capacity to influence. Over the years Thomas's own plans and aspirations (once fiercely independent) have drifted inexorably toward and ultimately fused with those of Towergate. Cullum's intense gravitational field exercises this remarkable pull repeatedly. We have also seen others succumb again and again. People, and able people in particular, have a propensity to be drawn into Peter Cullum's gravitational orbit. And this is a key point. Much of what is written about leadership and leadership development ignores or underplays one absolutely vital element: *the quality of the followers involved.*

Leading from the front

Cullum's achievement is remarkable because
stem from a fundamental rethink of the tra
that dominated insurance since before th
Cullum's new brand of financial m

Peter Cullum has led consolidati
the non-life insurance se
Towergate and Fo

Anyone with half a brain can lead the gullible or the dim, '*in the land of the blind etc...*' Exceptional leadership is fundamentally about inspiring and committing the highly capable. That is a different leadership challenge entirely, and Cullum is a master of it.

The interesting question of course is, 'how does he do it?'

Being an inveterate analyser, Thomas has thought long and hard about that question. He has asked it of numerous people at various levels within and outside of Towergate and even asked Cullum himself - to little avail, for the reasons outlined previously (it was worth a try.) Ultimately he has come to the conclusion that the simple answer, unfortunately, is that there is no simple answer. But there certainly are clues.

Almost inevitably, echoes from Peter Cullum's background and early experiences are pertinent. Born into a working-class family in East Anglia (his father was a bricklayer and his mother a factory worker) Cullum was a 'bright boy' who gained a place at one of the country's most admired and prestigious Grammar Schools.

Once there he became acutely aware of two things. First that he was mixing with boys who came from an entirely different social and economic strata altogether. As far as the impressionable young Cullum was concerned they emanated from a hitherto unexplored region of the social universe known as 'Affluenta Centauri!' This knocked him back initially but he soon came to the second of his realisations; that he was mentally faster than many of them. Being disinclined to hide any lights under bushels (never a Cullum strength!) and simply try to 'fit in' with this new, economically superior cohort, Cullum decided that if these boys were destined to be successful through average results and good contacts he would be successful through better results and hard work.

Despite the enormous differences in social and

economic backgrounds, and perhaps because of some inherent 'leadership' quality, present even then, Cullum made good friends with a number of his seriously affluent co-pupils. When invited to visit their homes he did not, as many impressionable youngsters may have, gaze around in serf-like wonder, but rather thought; 'If they can have this, I can have this.' The feeling was, Cullum freely admits, a mixture of both ambition and anger, a sort of 'hunger' to achieve that was tinged with deep feelings of resentment against the palpable differences of opportunity that a 'good start' offered. It is something that has remained with him ever since and forms the bedrock of his charitable trust, which is aimed at helping less advantaged youngsters reach their full potential.

It was during the later years of grammar school that the young Cullum, having made friends with a number of boys whose fathers happened to be senior managers in various financial and insurance companies, decided to skip university and get his feet onto the ladder of corporate progress. Cullum's move into the insurance sector, unlike the vast majority of employees who 'just happen into it', was a clear and calculated choice.

Once within the insurance sector Cullum realised that he needed to stand out in some significant way if he was to make real progress. The decision to skip university now meant that he needed to get himself professionally qualified. This he did with his customary 'no-half-measures' drive and focus. By age 20 he had achieved full ACII status and at age 21 was awarded his FCII.

Then, as if all that wasn't enough, in his early twenties and also newly married, Cullum decided to throw it all in and go to Business School, full time!

His resulting MBA (in Risk Analysis) from Cass Business School (formerly City Business School) included a final dissertation that challenged (successfully) one of the mainstays of then-accepted wisdom concerning aspects of human motivation. Ever the risk-taker, Cullum rejected any number of 'play-it-safe-and-quote-the-experts' topics in favour of the 'I'm-not-convinced-that-the-experts-have-got-it-right' option that would typify his intellectual approach from there on in. The dissertation was awarded a distinction.

Armed with his new qualification and, much more importantly, the deep insights that the whole research process had given him, Cullum went back into the Insurance sector more determined than ever to make a difference. The rest, as they say, is…

What drives an individual to make such choices and to take such risks? Is it mainly upbringing? Mainly inherent tendencies? Who knows? No-one does for sure.

There are indications however, albeit rather un-fashionable ones given the current 'anyone can become a great leader if they read the right books and follow the right plans' climate. Fashion in academic writing is a fickle business however and therefore we will look at some real-world practicalities.

The vast majority of people who have seen him in action recognise pretty quickly that Peter Cullum has the leadership 'X Factor'. Thomas has worked with other leaders who have been equally as bright, focused, ambitious (sometimes considerably more so, which may be revealing) and challenging as Peter Cullum. But Cullum has something extra, something that turns very good leaders into truly exceptional ones.

It is something we call 'Trustability'.

Trustability

Trustability is the capacity to generate an aura of competence and control that is so powerful it convinces all and sundry that they, with this leader at the helm, can succeed in the face of most odds. It is an extremely authoritative psychological energy and it constitutes a bona-fide definition of the much abused jargon-term 'empowerment'.

Trustability is capable of producing exceptional performances from sometimes unexceptional individuals. Churchill had it, Gandhi had it, Thomas's school rugby teacher had it, Peter Cullum has it.

Just as some soldiers are able to stand up in the face of a barrage of bullets and know they will not get hit so Cullum stands up in the face of business bullets. The demons of doubt simply do not exist. He has the innate ability to make everyone else believe in his inviolate nature also and to let him carry the burden of any worry.

Peter Cullum

The art of smart buying

When Peter Cullum and his colleagues first sat around his kitchen table in 1997 to plan the creation of Towergate, he was clear from the outset that acquisition was central to the strategy. What has been remarkable is the speed and intensity of the ambition and execution.

"We started with a plain sheet of ... " he says. "We thought ...

edge. We took our acquired market knowledge and then identified not just niches, but crevi...

Cull...
cla...

it was a straightforward process."

Insurers often outs...

However, Peter is the first to genuinely insist that it is people, the team, that matters most. They are the true 'assets' of the business, in fact people are the business. And he is not afraid to also admit that sometimes his judgement and management of people can go adrift.

This, if anything, could be considered as being Peter Cullum's potential 'weak spot'.

Despite his somewhat intimidating presence and ultra-direct communication style – he can and frequently does reduce grown men to tears – he can also be 'softer' on people than many others in positions of absolute power would be. Cullum will often put loyalty above performance for example and 'find a place' for committed and hard working individuals who have become borderline performers in a newly emerged and infinitely more demanding Towergate environment.

Also, a considerable amount of Cullum's time (and money) is devoted to the human side of the business. The Employee Benefit Trust is just one example, the Towergate Academy another. The work done on corporate social responsibility is equally important. Cullum appreciates that the team does not live off profit alone. This, again, marks out the exceptional leader from the simply good one.

The Psychology of Exceptional Leadership

The roots of exceptional leadership (like most things) are grounded in the structure of the human brain. Broadly speaking, our brains can be thought of as containing three distinct physiological structures.

First there is the extremely old (in evolutionary terms) 'Hindbrain' (the brainstem and pons) which is responsible for controlling 'basic' physiological functions such as breathing, sleeping, body temperature and digestion.

Second there is the 'Midbrain' or 'Limbic System' which sits over the Hindbrain and is heavily involved in processing emotions, particularly fear.

Lastly there is the 'Forebrain' or 'Higher Brain'

(cerebrum) which sits over both lower structures and is the seat of consciousness and thought.

Although all areas of the brain are highly interconnected, this structural distinction is a useful one.

It is the Midbrain or Limbic System that we will focus on here. The Limbic System is different from most other brain and body structures in that it is an 'open' system. Open systems, as their name implies, are susceptible to influence from outside of themselves, whereas 'closed' systems are not. Blood pressure for example is a closed system. My blood pressure cannot directly affect your blood pressure. If I have high blood pressure it's my problem not yours and you cannot 'catch' it from me. Emotions however, which are heavily controlled by the Limbic System, are a different kettle of fish

Structures of the Limbic system

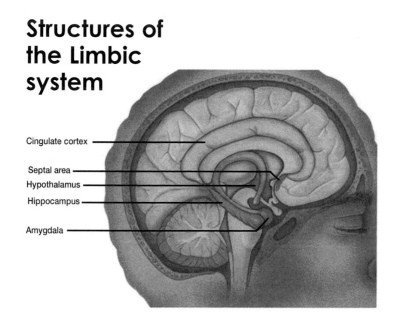

Cingulate cortex

Septal area
Hypothalamus
Hippocampus

Amygdala

altogether. Emotions are extremely 'contagious', witness the speed with which a yawn or giggle spreads through a group of children!

In many ways our emotional systems are continually 'monitoring' the environment in order to decide which setting they should be on. This is highly relevant to leadership as a key factor influencing a given individual's emotional state (the 'setting' of their own Limbic System) will be the emotional states (the Limbic System settings) of others, particularly important others. Young babies for example are expert at identifying and synchronising with the emotional states of their primary care-givers. Anxious care-givers send out subtle verbal and non-verbal signals (breathing rate, heart rate, voice pitch etc) which are registered by young babies and trigger similar emotions in them. On the bright side of course care-givers can also quiet fractious babies by rocking them gently and making calming noises. Essentially they are communicating the message that their Limbic System is set on 'all is well' and this commonly triggers (eventually!) a similar emotional state in the child.

And so it is with leadership. People's emotional states have a significant impact on their work performance and their emotional states will be heavily influenced by the emotional states of others, particularly important others such as senior managers. When the boss is 'off on one' everybody is on tenterhooks. When Peter Cullum is in a bad mood the sky goes black and livestock cower behind hedges!

The critical importance of emotion is also apparent when we break work performance down into its component parts. A useful framework is given below:

• Skills
• Knowledge
• Attitude

Poor or excellent performance can be analysed using these criteria. For example poor performance can sometimes be due to a lack of appropriate skills. Or it may be that an individual lacks certain knowledge. Of course it could be possible that they have all the necessary skills and knowledge required but lack the desire (attitude) to perform well. Any combination of factors can be at play but Attitude (emotion) is different from the others in a number of ways. Firstly emotions, unlike skills and knowledge, have a relatively short 'shelf-life'. Skills, such as the ability to ride a bicycle or swim, once mastered, stay with us virtually for the whole of our lives. It is similar with useful or important knowledge (the majority of people can recall the birth dates of their parents long after their parents' demise).

Attitudes are incredibly volatile however, individuals can move from respecting their bosses to despising them in the space of a single email!

Attitudes, particularly positive attitudes, are also rather short-lived (unfortunately) and require fairly regular 'top up' in order to be maintained. Effective telesales managers understand this fact all too well and frequently start the sales day with some variety of 'spirit-lifting-we-are-the greatest' type of activity (usually with varying degrees of success) aimed at getting their people 'fired up'.

The emotions most commonly associated with high performance at work are; *Pride* (in the organisation and its products and services) *Trust* (in the organisation and its managers) *Confidence* (in their own ability to do the jobs required of them) *Enjoyment* (of the work and the working environment) and *Growth* (the feeling that they are not stagnating as people).

Achieving, and more importantly maintaining these positive emotions, is not an easy task. In fact it is immeasurably easier to generate their opposites. An unnecessarily critical email, boring meeting, confused message or perceived slight can bring the whole lot tumbling down. Because emotions (particularly positive ones) can be so volatile, managers need to be aware that they will be crucial factors in 'setting the emotional benchmark' at work, as our brief exploration of the human brain above has hopefully shown.

Since the creation of Towergate, Cullum has insisted that the Company has soul. He always wanted CSR (Corporate Social Responsibility) to mean something and not just the Cause Related Marketing that creams off 30p in the £1 to the advertising agencies that develop the campaigns! Cullum wants staff to be able to hold their heads up high. Towergate, its staff and its customers, have between them raised over £100,000 per annum for good causes in the UK. There is no doubt that this has had enormously positive effects.

Towergate Partnership donates £500k to the Norfolk Hospice, Tapping House.
Left to right: Tessa Scott, Chairman, Norfolk Hospice, Tapping House,
Peter Cullum, Executive Chairman, Towergate Partnership
David Praill, CEO, Help the Hospices
Janet Doyle, Chief Executive, Norfolk Hospice, Tapping House

Exceptional Trustability

The stages on which exceptional leadership may be played out can vary enormously in both scope and consequence, from world wars to school rugby football matches, but Trustability runs through them all.

The simple fact is that people believe Cullum has the ability and drive necessary to succeed in whatever business venture he tackles. They believe that although he is not risk-averse he is not reckless either (holding an MBA in risk management also helps!) People also believe that if Cullum succeeds, they will succeed too, that they will receive their fair share of any benefits.

When people choose to follow an individual on an uncertain commercial journey they are essentially 'out-sourcing' their economic and personal futures. This is a big decision to make and intelligent people will only make that decision if they have absolute belief in the capabilities of the individual up front. People trust Peter Cullum. They trust his integrity and they trust his ability to succeed and win. They trust him on a wide range of levels and consequently (ourselves included) are happy to throw their lot in with him.

Exceptional Trustability is at the core of exceptional leadership. Thomas believes it is as simple (and complex) as that. He also believes that exceptional Trustability (which involves generating extremely high levels of perceived competence and integrity) is essentially 'unteachable'. It can be 'drawn out' of people but it cannot be 'put in'. People either have it, or the innate capability to develop it, or they do not. Most people do not. If this seems a somewhat depressing or even conflicting assertion given the plethora of books which suggests that leadership is a highly learnable skill, we reiterate that we are talking about exceptional leadership here and, as with all instances of exceptional abilities, they are exceptional by virtue of the fact that they are rare.

Exceptional leaders are rare for a number of reasons. First there are the differing cognitive and emotional factors involved. An individual may be extremely competent intellectually and professionally yet lack the personal qualities (drive, vision, integrity, ability to motivate etc.) necessary to generate high levels of Trustability in others. Conversely they may have the personal qualities necessary but be perceived as lacking the intellectual or professional ones. Having the whole kybosh together in one individual is a rare thing indeed.

It is not all about 'Nature' and genes however, we cannot ignore the role that chance life experiences, 'Nurture', plays in drawing out or inhibiting the development of latent talents. Peter Cullum's decision to leave a secure and successful career in order to take on Economic for example was partly influenced by chance events. If circumstances had been different he may have stayed put and simply moved further up the corporate hierarchy. We seriously doubt however that the challenges to be faced there would have been as transformative as those involved in the turn-around of Economic and the subsequent establishment of Towergate. As with all latent talent, deprived of a facilitative environment it will not flourish. Prior to the Economic/Towergate journey Peter Cullum was an extremely effective leader. Along the way he became an exceptional one.

Towergate will always be a very good company and will, in all probability, continue to outperform its peers. With leaders such as Peter Cullum on song it is a truly great company.

Key Lessons: Exceptional leadership, by definition, is exceptionally rare. Both Dyer and Thomas freely admit that they could not have led and managed

Towergate anywhere as effectively as Cullum has (nowhere near, to be frank). Our trick was to latch on to him early and go with the flow!
Exceptional leadership is indeed a rarity but effective leadership is necessary at all levels within an organisation. Effective leadership is essentially about trust, honesty and respect. Senior management must identify those individuals who have real leadership potential and systematically develop them.

Our final advice on the topic of leadership is this: wherever possible, work for an organisation that has an exceptional leader at its helm!

Wired?

The basic thinking that lies behind the question of whether leaders are 'born' or 'made' raises a number of other interesting conundrums.

Consider the following for example:

1. *You wish to sell your shares in six months time. A friend who dabbles in financial markets advises that you should switch them from ABC plc to DEF plc. You do not do so. Six months later you find that had you switched your shares you would have made an extra profit of £5,000.*

On a scale of one-to-ten, how disappointed would you feel?

2. *You wish to sell your shares in six months time. A friend who dabbles in financial markets advises that you should switch them from ABC plc to DEF plc. You do so. Six months later you find that had you left your shares where they were you*

would have made an extra profit of £5,000.

On a scale of one-to-ten, how disappointed would you feel?

You would no doubt feel some degree of dis-appointment had either situation arisen. But would you be equally disappointed in each case?

Psychological studies consistently show that individuals feel much worse when placed in scenario 2 than they do in scenario 1. This is entirely illogical as in both instances people have 'lost' an opportunity to make an additional £5,000 profit on their shares.

So why do people feel so much worse in scenario 2 than they do in scenario 1?

Maybe you have noticed the key difference?

In scenario 2 we *take action* and this action leads to a 'loss' of £5,000.

In scenario 1 it is our *inaction* that leads to the same 'loss'.

The problem is that *loss from action registers much more keenly than loss from inaction.*

Consequently there is a sort of psychological 'cost' involved when we consider taking any action that involves some degree of uncertainty. Because of this 'cost of action', the fear that we will do something that doesn't work out, we require greater justification for taking action than we do for not taking action.

It is psychologically easier to not make a decision involving risk than to make one. It is psychologically easier to leave a difficult but risky situation alone than to do something about it (especially if it has been that way for some time).

When faced with real choices, choices that involve a degree of uncertainty, doing nothing is much more comfortable than doing something.

These and other 'irrational' psychological factors

influence a variety of management and leadership actions.

Again consider the following:

1. *You wish to purchase a new electric kettle. The model you have decided upon is in stock at your local electrical retailer (one mile from your home)and is priced at £50. As you set off to purchase the kettle you notice that an alternative retailer is offering exactly the same model for £25 as part of a new-store promotion. The alternative retailer is eleven miles from your home.*

   Would you be prepared to drive the extra distance in order to purchase the kettle at the reduced price?

   Jot down the probability that you would drive the extra distance in order to purchase the item at the reduced price.

2. *You wish to purchase a new High Definition plasma TV. The model you have decided upon is in stock at your local electrical retailer (one mile from your home)and is priced at £2,795. As you set off to purchase the TV you notice that an alternative retailer is offering exactly the same model for £2,770 as part of a new-store promotion. The alternative retailer is eleven miles from your home.*

   Would you be prepared to drive the extra distance in order to purchase the TV at the reduced price?
   Jot down the probability that you would drive the extra distance in order to purchase the item at the reduced price.

When we use this exercise as part of the Towergate Academy Development Programme delegates see only one of the two scenarios described above.

Of those who see the 'kettle' version, virtually 100% say they would be prepared to drive the extra distance in order to purchase the item at the reduced price.

Of those who see the 'TV' version fewer than 5% say they would be prepared to drive the extra distance in order to purchase the item at the reduced price.

Again this is illogical. If it is worth travelling the extra distance to save £25 in scenario 1 why is it not worth travelling the same distance to save the same £25 in scenario 2?

Delegates commonly come up with a variety of spurious excuses and illogical justifications for not being prepared to travel exactly the same distance to save exactly the same amount of money in scenario 2 as virtually everyone is prepared to do in Scenario 1. Had they been presented with scenario1 of course these people would no doubt (as everyone else does) have taken a completely different view.

So what is happening here?

The basic problem is known as 'anchoring'.

Saving £25 on a purchase of £50 registers, correctly, as a serious reduction owing to the fact that we 'anchor' on the £50 original price.

In contrast a saving of £25 anchored against a purchase price of £2,795 just doesn't seem worth the effort.

In reality exactly the same effort is required to make a profit of £25 in both instances. If it's worth driving the extra miles to save £25 in one instance it should be worth doing so in the other. Shouldn't it?

If we were utterly rational beings yes, but we are not utterly rational beings.

Capitalising on such thinking is a bedrock of the Towergate method as expounded by Peter Cullum. Too many professions and industries are driven by illogical pricing or distribution methodologies. Cullum has consistently pointed out the organisational equivalents of the 'eleven miles for £25' example given above yet there are still those who fail to grasp it.

There are numerous examples of similar (and even more debilitating) human peculiarities documented in the annals of experimental psychology. All managers should be aware of them. Systems-based theories of management often underestimate the devastating impact such peculiarities and irrationalities can have on the most logical and best-laid of organisational plans.

> **Key Lessons: human beings are highly susceptible to distortions of thinking. The more we understand their devious machinations the better we can avoid their more negative consequences. Practice in logical thinking skills (e.g. materials developed by people such as Edward de Bono) can improve our ability to make more rational decisions.**

Octagonal holes and hexagonal pegs?

Whether we like it or not (we are beginning to accept the notion at least) a significant proportion of our behaviours and predispositions appear to be 'hard-wired' in. The ways in which we are susceptible to systematic distortions of thinking described above are an example. Psychological research increasingly suggests that aspects of personality may be significantly influenced by genetics also. A recent study of identical and non-identical twins for example found that where one identical twin was entrepreneurial the other was much more likely to be entrepreneurial also than were the same-sex brother or sister of a non-identical entrepreneurial twin. As identical twins share one hundred percent of their genes in common and non-identical twins on average share only fifty percent, is this clear evidence of a genetic predisposition toward entrepreneurial behaviour in certain individuals? Who knows? Time will no doubt tell. There is an old adage which counsels that in order to live a long and healthy life the single most important thing we should all do is choose our parents very carefully. Ongoing psychological research suggests that this adage may apply to a wide range of personal attributes too. If this seems a tad 'deterministic' we would ask that you reserve judgement for the moment.

While fully accepting that the concept of 'genetic determinism' hasn't had a very auspicious history to date it is also fair to say that there is a significant downside to the 'anyone can become anything they truly set their hearts on' movement too.

Experience shows us that people clearly have different predispositions and talents and the ideal situation for any organisation is to arrange things in order that they are able to play to their particular strengths. When individuals are enabled to do what they are really good at doing everyone wins. At Towergate we consistently attempt to apply a sound approach of matching 'pegs' to 'holes.'

A central challenge facing most organisations is finding practical ways in which this 'matching of talents to organisational requirements' can be integrated with suitable remuneration and career development opportunities. In a previous life as a design engineer Thomas witnessed the repeated application of pay and promotion systems that conspired to produce the direct opposite of what was best for the organisation.

Exceptionally talented engineers would commonly rise to the summits of their respective pay and promotion scales quite rapidly and the only opportunities then available for further progress involved transferring from the engineering spine to the 'general management' spine. Unfortunately the qualities that make someone an exceptional engineer do not necessarily make them an exceptional manager (in fact you could credibly argue the opposite). Thus the organisation often lost out on three accounts. It lost the services of an excellent engineer, frequently acquired an average or even poor general manager and it laid out a considerable amount of money for the privilege of facilitating the exchange!

It is frequently similar with management and leadership development. Experience shows that a significant proportion of individuals engaged in such programmes possess few if any of the key attributes required for really effective leadership. These are not the sorts of attributes that can be 'injected' into individuals, such as project management or financial planning skills, but attributes that can only be cultivated from within. Attributes such as courage in the face of unfavourable odds, self-belief, innovation, determination, sociability and even 'charisma'. We can certainly nurture the seedlings of such attributes but we cannot seed them. The truth, palatable or otherwise, is that such attributes are not naturally present in everyone, certainly not to the level required for truly effective leadership to be developed. And that is no tragedy either. We must not lose sight of the fact that effective organisations are not comprised solely of leaders (thank heavens!). Effective organisations need people to put flesh on the vision, people who will go out and actually build the edifice.

Many (most?) effective leaders are not 'doers' but 'dreamers' and if there are insufficient people willing and able to follow their dream then they are done for. Leaders without followers are powerless just as followers without leaders are rudderless. Each feeds off the other and is strengthened by the other.

We forget at our peril that there is equal glory in making the dream a reality as there is in dreaming it in the first place. The preference for 'thinking over doing' so evident in the exponential growth of 'higher education' and corresponding decline in 'vocational training' (the terms themselves are instructional) has profound implications for both business and society. Technical expertise, be it in the fields of manufacturing, computing, underwriting or claims handling is central to the long-term health of any business or indeed any national economy and we must not lose sight of this fact. In the UK for example we hardly ever teach our children even the basics of personal financial management. Is it any wonder therefore that we currently (2007) have a national personal debt problem of over £1 trillion?

Unfortunately senior managers can, and very often do, become seriously detached from the core (boring?) activities of their businesses. This is dangerous.

The popular UK television programme 'Back to the Floor' which requires senior executives (often the CEO) to spend a period of time at 'the sharp end' of their businesses invariably, and totally predictably, generates 'great revelations' for all concerned. The fact that it requires participation in a television programme to reintroduce these executives to their own fundamental business operations speaks volumes in itself. Towergate's senior management are actively encouraged to talk to staff, to look at the letters generated for customers, to read claims files, to try the systems for themselves.

A good number of organisations, which means a good number of senior managers, would benefit from re-discovering their genuine appreciation (and not simply inserting the ubiquitous 'our customer-facing people are our greatest asset' statement into every annual report) for the 'key workers' within their businesses, the people who actually get the fundamental things done. This appreciation should particularly apply to those with exceptional 'technical' or 'operational' skills. As with the engineering example above, many such individuals hit a promotion or pay ceiling fairly early on and are then faced with few if any attractive options for the future. Waiting for the section head to be promoted or leave (or die) or moving into 'general management', if those are the only perceived options for 'progress' available, or thinking about moving out of the organisation altogether. All inevitably lead to a loss of motivation and a drop in performance.

The most effective way to get people to do a good job is to give them a good job to do; and that is one that best matches their natural talents and dispositions. It is well to remember that organisations need (require?) only a few exceptional Chiefs to succeed ('too many cooks … etc ') but exceptional Indians are a different matter altogether, an organisation can never have too many of them. Not everyone necessarily aspires to leadership positions and some who do are not particularly suited to the role. There is no disgrace in preferring to do rather than tell. Organisations (and society for that matter) must ensure that the people who, in the philosopher Bertrand Russell's telling phrase, prefer to '*move matter about in space**' rather than to talk about it, are genuinely valued for the essential contribution they make. We are all wired differently, not desperately wanting to be the boss is OK, in fact it's absolutely vital!

> **Key Lessons: people work best when they play to their strengths. Wherever possible place people in roles that suit their particular personalities and interests. Never forget the potentially 'invisible' staff who do the underlying work that actually keeps the business going.**

News at Ten

Ask a hundred people at random what they consider to be the most frustrating and debilitating problem in their

---

*Russell's full remark on the nature of work was; 'Work is of two kinds: 1. Moving matter about in space. 2. Telling other people to do so. The first is unpleasant and poorly paid, the second is pleasant and highly paid.'

organisation and at least eighty percent (usually ninety plus) will give you the same answer.

Communication.
By which they mean poor communication.
Everybody says it, everywhere, all of the time.

'Nobody tells us anything.' 'We don't get to know anything until it's too late.' 'I don't know what they really want from us.' 'We keep getting mixed messages.' 'Nobody tells us the really important stuff.'

Sound familiar? Probably. So what do people mean when they say these and other things about the 'poor communications' in their organisations? That the organisation does not communicate anything? No. It is impossible to not-communicate.

Not-communicating communicates precisely that!

The vast majority of organisations understand the importance of effective communication and   seek to 'communicate' with their employees through various mechanisms including company newsletters, intranet bulletins, regular team briefings and so on. These are always well intentioned and often well executed efforts, but many fail to appreciate that they are directed toward a diverse audience with quite different ideas of what 'good communication' is and widely varying agendas of what they want to hear. Informal research suggests for example that many people dread the weekly/fortnightly/monthly team briefing from the boss. The following (actual) comments are not unrepresentative:

'Boring.' 'Too many figures.' 'Didn't understand it.' 'Same as the last one.' 'Another arse-kicking session.' 'All jargon.'

Such comments are instructive even when we accept (rightly) that a proportion will probably have been made by organisational cynics. The core problem is that derisive comments such as those above usually follow communication activities that are set up for the sole purpose of '*communicating.*' Just like scheduled news broadcasts with fixed time slots, those delivering such sessions will 'fill the time' with something, newsworthy or otherwise. As an anonymous wit wryly observed many years ago, it is truly amazing that just enough 'news' happens each and every day to completely fill the newspapers! Because organisations understand 'the importance of communication' they often fall into the trap of 'communicating for communication's sake' and end up boring vast swathes of their staff.

It is also a curious fact that, despite the importance we all place on effective communication, how few, and particularly how few aspiring senior managers, are taught the art of communicating effectively, including of course the vital art of presenting to groups.

The ability to present a business case effectively is a required skill of most Board members. Hopefully they come with particular specialist skills also but their ability to present effectively will be taken for granted. After all, the elites of the Roman Empire regarded oratory skills as absolutely fundamental to any individual occupying any position of power – maybe we could learn from them.

What most people actually want from the organisation is not 'communication' but news, information that has some emotional resonance, information that impacts on their core hopes and fears.

Again different people will have different agendas but a number of themes are common, E.g. (in no particular order of importance):

- How safe is my job?
- Is what I do seen as being important and valued by managers?
- What is the standing of our company within our sector? (Am I working for an admired and respected outfit?)
- Are there any plans afoot that could have an impact on me personally?
  (Not saying there are no such plans afoot is not enough, rumour networks are inevitably negative and apocalyptic. Letting people know what is NOT planned can pay dividends too, especially in times of change or uncertainty.)
- What are we doing that is innovative or different from our competitors?
- How is the company doing?
  (This has to be handled with some care. Lauding exceptional financial performance for example, although the intention may be to boost feelings of security and praise staff performance, can lead people to wonder 'how much of this money will I actually see?')
- What and who is new?
- What are the possibilities for me in this company?

'Formal' corporate communications can benefit greatly from acknowledging the accepted wisdom on formal performance appraisals; that they should NOT be about day-to-day performance, this must be addressed by line managers on a continuing basis, but should focus instead on aspirations, emotions and core aims. Effective corporate communication is about quality not quantity and it is most effective when it addresses the emotional concerns that power rumour networks. Towergate has a chatty, approachable style. ANYONE can call or email Peter Cullum.

Key Lessons: effective communication is essential to all organisations. Many organisations try hard at 'communicating' but often fail through 'over-communicating' or by communicating information that no-one is really interested in. People respond to genuine 'news' and to communications that address their core interests, aspirations and fears. Have a genuine 'open door' policy on communication, allow people the opportunity to ask the questions (anonymously if necessary) that interest or concern them. Communication channels should be as open as possible both 'top down' and 'bottom up'.

Speaking in Tongues

Certain forms of 'Higher Education' appear to have a curious effect on some individuals. It makes them talk crap.

Admittedly it's often impressive crap, but it's crap none the less.

The mangled language and buzzwords of 'Management Speak' hit the headlines in the UK in November 2006 via an 'Investors In People' survey which found that 54% of UK employees consider such jargon to be a serious barrier to effective communication (the real percentage was most probably higher, staff are often reluctant to confess to such opinions, for obvious reasons.)

Among the particularly risible offenders identified were gems such as:

- 'Blue-sky thinking.'
- 'Getting our ducks in a row.'
- 'Joined-up thinking.'
- 'On the runway.'

- 'Pushing the envelope.'
- 'Reading from the same hymn sheet.'
- 'Banging on the same drum.'

Such examples are gut-wrenchingly awful but most sane people tend to see them for what they are, the verbal tics of the cognitively limited (never expressed to the faces of the protagonists concerned of course, again for obvious reasons!)

But language-mangling frequently goes further than the merely laughable, it can have serious consequences right across the organisation, and it is certainly not a modern phenomenon.

In a collection of essays entitled 'Politics and the English Language' (1946) the writer George Orwell lampooned the use of pompous and confusing language. One of his most telling examples involves a translation of the passage from Ecclesiastes which we used as the opener to this book. Orwell took the original and rewrote it in a style that would not look out of place in many of today's corporate reports. The original version and Orwell's rewrite are given below:

> *'I returned and saw under the sun, that the race is not to the swift, nor the battle to the strong, neither yet bread to the wise, nor yet riches to men of understanding, nor yet favour to men of skill; but time and chance happeneth to them all.'*

Here it is rewritten in what Orwell called 'modern English':

> *'Objective considerations of contemporary phenomena compel the conclusion that success or failure in competitive activities exhibits no tendency to be commensurate with innate capacity, but that a*

considerable element of the unpredictable must invariably be taken into account.'

While both (we think at least) are attempting to express the same truths, the original has (for us) very strong emotional content and a certain lyrical beauty. The rewrite stimulates a powerful desire to 'engage in acts of voluntary self-termination' (to use the lingo).

Below we offer a few examples of real corporate statements taken from one of the many anti-jargon Internet sites that have sprung up in the spirit of the 'Dilbert' cartoon strip so beloved of 'ordinary workers.'

Similarly, inter-divisional teamwork must work within parameters which address the need for developing congruent business partnerships.

Nevertheless, inter-divisional teamwork interacts synergistically with change management in pinpointing the values that individuals add to key client processes.

Moreover, devolution of profit and revenue responsibility means that management must concentrate on the operational imperative of meeting trans-national and trans-industrial competition.

As far as we can see the first statement is an attempt at getting everyone to work together toward a common goal (to 'sing from the same hymn sheet!') the other two are way beyond our combined cryptographic talents.

Language is an extremely powerful mediator of thought. Clear language encourages clear thinking.

Unfortunately there is often a marked tendency to equate complex language use with intelligence: 'the bigger the words, the bigger the brain'.

This can be really damaging. When people, through no fault of their own, fail to understand unnecessarily complex language (whether written or spoken) they frequently blame themselves, '*I must be thick*' when in fact the problem lies with the *sender* and not the receiver.

Peter Cullum is an extremely clear communicator (ask anyone!) and those who have experienced a 'Culluming' know exactly what is expected of them. He does not use bullshit or jargon and he does not camouflage his meaning. He uses everyday words and phrases to simplify concepts and focus people's attention on the practicalities of action (*Where are we now? 'Where do we want to be? How are we going to get from here to there?*). He also insists on file notes of all meetings, confirming action points, to be issued within 24 hours. No ambiguity, just calls for action by whom and by when. The sort of stuff ITT was doing 30 years ago but so many have now forgotten. With Cullum there is no obfuscation of meaning (if you get our point) responsibility or intent, consequently there are no hiding places either!

It is a fact of life of course that all groups, from street rappers to existential philosophers, inevitably develop their own 'private languages', the use of which signifies membership of the club (recall the confusing language of the investment bankers encountered early in the Towergate journey). It is not surprising therefore that many managers are prone to this tendency also, but the dangers involved are three-fold.

First there are potentially divisive and damaging 'them and us' consequences if managers consistently employ different forms of speech from everyone else.

Second, and why this should be the case is interesting, most of the jargon that has evolved within 'Management

Speak' tends to sound hysterically comical to everyone else and this doesn't help in the vitally important management credibility stakes!

Lastly, and probably most importantly, unnecessarily complex language can and frequently does overcomplicate what are in fact fairly straightforward concepts and ideas. Most people, in mortal fear of appearing dim, are wary of seeking clarification on confusing utterances (particularly when in the company of people senior to themselves) and usually keep quiet, nod sagely along with everyone else, and then go away and try to make the best sense they can of what is required of them.

The emergence and use of technical terms and specialist shorthand is virtually inevitable in any profession and it is frequently constructive, but laughable jargon and pretentious pseudo-speak are most certainly not. So, beware those whom a past mentor of ours once described as constituting 'the eloquent incompetents!'

Lastly, in concluding this brief discussion of an immensely important area of management behaviour (and we mean that) we humbly offer our version of a chapter of the 'Bullshit Bible' that has graced the internet blogs of many of the world's disaffected employees over the past few years. We hope you enjoy it (and maybe even leave it where a culpable manager may 'find' it!)

GENESIS (2)

In the beginning was the Plan,
then followed the Assumptions.
And the Assumptions were without form,
and the Plan was without substance.

And darkness was upon the face of the Workers.

And they spoke amongst themselves saying,
"This is crap, it stinks."

And the Workers went to the Supervisors and said unto them,
"This is a complete pail of dung and it truly reeks."

And the Supervisors went unto the Middle Managers saying,
"It is a container of excrement and is very strong indeed,
such that none may abide by it."

And the Middle Managers went unto the Divisional Directors saying,
"It is a vessel of fertilizer and none may abide its strength."

And the Divisional Directors spoke among themselves,
saying to one another,
"It containeth that which aids plant development,
and it is very strong."

And the Divisional Directors went to the Vice Presidents saying unto them,
"It promoteth vegetative enlargement and it is very powerful indeed."

And the Vice Presidents went to the President and said unto him,

"It shall bring into being significant upward curvature in organic growth, and it is strategically robust."

And the President looked upon the Plan and said that it was good.

And verily the Plan did become Company Policy ...

And that is how most shit happens.

Key Lessons: ensure your communications (written and spoken) are as clear and direct as possible. Avoid unnecessary jargon and buzzwords. Clear speaking and writing encourages clear thinking. If you receive a message (written or spoken) that you find difficult to understand don't assume that the problem resides with you. Question it. Take every opportunity to further develop your communication and presentation skills. Presentation Skills training is one of the most effective (and terrifying!) management and leadership development tools available.

Next Steps?

The only way to predict the future is to create it.

Anonymous

What's next for Towergate? Who can tell? Currently (June 2007) the company is a very different entity from the one we envisaged it would be just ten years ago. A tremendous amount has changed and our progress to date has been very rapid indeed. But we are not complacent. We have learned an important lesson, it is that the key to ongoing progress rests in ongoing reinvention and recreation and that is not about doing the same things that everyone else does but doing them better, but challenging accepted 'givens' and creating new and innovative approaches to doing business.

Andrew Sibbald, Managing Director at Lexicon Partners (sole advisers on all significant Towergate purchases and financing) who has been involved with Peter Cullum ever since the sale of Economic Insurance to Hiscox, suggests that Towergate is currently 'chapter six of a twelve-chapter book.' He may very well be correct. We ourselves doubt that 'the book' will contain fewer 'chapters'. Our perspective is that it may very well turn out to be an encyclopaedia. But again, we will not tempt fate!

Sibbald and his Lexicon colleague Stuart Britton cite the willingness of Towergate managers and staff to 'expect the unexpected' and to accept that the future will be recreated continuously as being a core strength underpinning the success of the business. Towergate staff need to embrace change, to quote Sibbald, like 'business commandos.'

Sibbald also cites the crucial importance of trust and personal relationships in cementing substantial deals. Just as we learned in the early days of Towergate that there needed to be some sort of personal 'bond' between ourselves and the owners of the businesses we purchased, Sibbald stresses the continuing importance of this factor at all levels. And in Sibbald's view of Towergate, 'the best is yet to come.'

How does Peter Cullum see the future? In the final interview for this book he stressed time and again that the business truly is all about teamwork, focus, innovation, hard work and cooperation. He appreciates that he is an extremely demanding boss (what successful leader isn't?) and that he asks, and will continue to ask, a great deal of people. But he also believes that asking a great deal of people is what ultimately helps make people great. He is immensely proud of what people have achieved at Towergate and he views the various accolades he has been awarded over the years, including UK Entrepreneur of the Year, Dealmaker of the Year, an honorary Doctorate from Cass Business School, as being accepted on their behalf. The Company itself has been awarded UK Private Company of the Year 2007 by ACQ Magazine.

And as to the future? Cullum has learned from experience that, just as 'the past is a foreign country', the future has no known geography, and that the only way to predict it is to attempt to create it. In pursuance of this belief he has established a Foundation to help young people with no

Professional Broking December 2006

Andy Homer CEO and Peter Cullum

Double Take

"We're mainly from an underwriting background – we've got the scars on our backs and we know how it feels to lose money at underwriting."

"An IPO is not an exit... that would only be another pit stop for us."

advantages fulfil their true potential and he has also set up (and persuaded serious money-men to contribute also) an Entrepreneurial Fund that will provide start-up finance for MBA students who have highly innovative (but also realistic!) plans for business creation.

Cullum's own perspective on the future of Towergate is that it will reinvent itself again and again, he has no doubts about that. Some people, to use his 'Towergate Voyage' analogy, will 'stay on the bus' while others will choose to get off of their own volition. A few may warrant the attention of the conductor!

But the bus will inevitably keep moving, even when the destination board simply reads; '*Forward*.'

Masterclass February 2007

Growing concerns

"I am anti monolithic structures. We allow the business a lot of autonomy because we want to nurture the entrepreneurial spirit, not squeeze it out of them."

"£700m turnover grows to £1.8bn. 2,000 staff increase to 3,650. One hundred acquisitions multiply to 121. Average acquisition value rockets from £25m to £180m. Now Europe's largest independent intermediary, Towergate has executed phenomenal growth in the last 12 months – and chairman Peter Cullum's voracious appetite for acquisition shows no sign of abating."

END NOTE

Hopefully this brief account of the trials and tribulations involved in a journey that began with the buyout of a small insurance company in Sittingbourne and currently finds its protagonists at the leading edge of a quite revolutionary change within the insurance industry itself has provided some useful insights into the realities of life at the business coal-face.

There have indeed been periods of considerable panic along the way; a great deal of passion, which remains to the present time, and also the realisation that people have far more power to create worthwhile change than they sometimes realise.

It has been an exhilarating roller-coaster of a ride so far and there will no doubt be ample heart-stopping surprises, unexpected diversions and stimulating challenges as we go forward.

We would like to take this final opportunity to sincerely thank all those who have made the journey possible, the people who make Towergate the company it is today. Exceptional vision and leadership have indeed been present from the very beginning, but that would have amounted to little without the exceptional people who have rallied to the call and made that vision a reality.

The Founders of Towergate

From left to right: Paul Dyer, Peter Cullum, Tony Proverbs